Business Strategy

Business Strategy

Second Edition

John Grieve Smith

Basil Blackwell

First published 1985 jointly by Basil Blackwell Ltd
108 Cowley Road, Oxford, OX4 1JF, UK and The Economist
Publications Ltd, 40 Duke Street, London W1M 5DG

Reprinted 1987

Second Edition 1990 by Basil Blackwell Ltd only.

Basil Blackwell, Inc.
3 Cambridge Center
Cambridge, Massachusetts 02142, USA

British Library Cataloguing in Publication Data

A CIP catalogue record for this book is available from the
British Library.

Library of Congress Cataloguing in Publication Data

Grieve Smith, John.
  Business strategy/John Grieve Smith, − 2nd ed.
    p.   cm.
  Includes bibliographical references.
  ISBN 0-631-17738-8 (pbk)
  1. Corporate planning. 2. Strategic planning. I. Title.
HD30.28.G75   1990
658.4′012−dc20
                                          89-18283
                                               CIP

Typeset in 11 on 12 pt Times
by Setrite Typesetters Limited Hong Kong
Printed in Great Britain by T.J. Press (Padstow) Ltd, Padstow, Cornwall

Contents

      The Concept of Balance   87
      The BCG Approach   89
      Matrix Approach Developments   96
      Portfolio Objectives   99
      The Role of Portfolio Analysis   100

7   *Competitive Strategy*   103

      Structural Analysis   103
      Successful Strategies   108
      Strategies for Different Types of Industries   110
      Defensive and Offensive Strategies   115
      Turnaround Strategies   117

8   *Strategic Planning*   121

      Corporate Planning   122
      Hierarchy of Plans   126
      Investment Planning   129
      Planning in the Large Integrated Firm   134
      Computer Models   139

9   *Financial Evaluation*   145

      Evaluation and Forecasting   145
      Investment Evaluation   148
      Evaluation Techniques   154
      Evaluation of Strategic Options   164

10   *State Enterprises and Public Utilities*   168

      Purposes of State Ownership   169
      Forms of Public Ownership   171
      Management Features   172
      Relations with Government   173
      Strategic Constraints   176
      Public Utilities   181

11   *Small, High-technology Firms*   184

      Formulating Strategy   185
      Relationships with Large Firms   193
      Strategic Guidelines   195

Preface

I should like to thank the Foundation for Management Education for their financial and moral support in making possible my transition from industry to the academic world by awarding me an Industrial Management Teaching Fellowship at the City University Business School. I should also like to thank Professor John Treasure and his colleagues at CUBS for welcoming me there and encouraging me to teach their MBA students. This book was conceived because I found what seemed to be a lack of a suitable introduction to business strategy for managers or students coming fresh to the subject. It reflects two beliefs based on experience. The first is that the more abstract the approach, the less likely it is to be adopted or to be effective in practice. The second is that industries and firms differ widely in their strategic problems, and the approach adopted must be tailored to the needs of the individual firm in the particular circumstances of the moment.

I am most grateful to Peter Evans and Tony Sweeney for reading the manuscript and making numerous constructive comments on the text (but they are, of course, in no way responsible for the eventual outcome). I should also like to thank Denise Prosser of Robinson College for all her help in making it possible to complete the task.

Preface to Second Edition

I should like to thank Vivien Fleck for letting me use the results of our joint studies of business strategy in small, high-technology firms as the basis for chapter 11 and Lesley Haird for helping me prepare the new edition for the press.

1

The Concept of Strategy

Strategy as an area of management is concerned with the general direction and long-term policy of the enterprise as distinct from short-term tactics and day-to-day operations. Hence the strategy of a business may be defined as its long-term objectives and the general means by which it intends to achieve them.

We shall be concerned primarily with business enterprises, whether in the private sector or state-owned, but many of the concepts and techniques involved can also be applied to other organisations, such as government agencies, educational institutions, research organisations, etc.

An important feature of business strategy is the need to consider the reactions of others to any initiative taken by the firm, particularly the reactions of its competitors, but also of bodies such as trade unions, national and local governments and regulating agencies. In this respect there is a close analogy with the need in military strategy to assess the possible reaction of the enemy; and neglect of this consideration is an important source of business failure. A good example is Laker Airways' apparent failure to think through their major competitors' possible counter-moves to their attacks on the transatlantic fare structure. They started a war they could not win and ended up in the hands of the receivers.

Although the systematic study of business strategy is a relatively recent development, the existence of such strategies dates back to the earliest commercial and industrial ventures. Many successful businesses have been guided by strategies derived from experience or intuition rather than analysis, or have even achieved success without any explicit strategy at all. But many more unsuccessful businesses have come to grief on the basis of strategies similarly conceived.

Whether they were successful depended on whether the strategic concept fitted the opportunities and circumstances of the time rather than on how it was conceived. A systematic approach to formulating strategy may not be a guarantee of success, nor an intuitive approach a guarantee of failure. Nevertheless, as business life becomes more complex, the chances of success depend increasingly on adopting strategies that are firmly based on an accurate and realistic assessment of the firm's position and the opportunities open to it.

Since the nature of strategic decision-making differs widely from case to case, so too must the approach and techniques for tackling them. A systematic discussion of possible approaches and techniques can, however, enable practising managers or students of business policy to take advantage of other people's experience and ideas in tackling such problems, and hence to deal with their own problems more effectively. Liddell Hart starts his history of military strategy with Bismarck's aphorism, 'Fools say they learn by experience. I prefer to profit by others' experience.'[1] The same might be said of the virtues of studying industrial strategy.

In recent years discussion of planning and strategy has gone through a rapid succession of phases, reflecting changes partly in approach, partly only of nomenclature. First 'corporate planning' was the answer, then 'strategic planning', only to give way to 'strategic management'. The first emphasised the need for a comprehensive plan covering all aspects of the business, particularly the financial aspect; the second placed greater stress on the evolution of a long-term strategy; and the last put most weight on designing the organisation of the firm to respond to a rapidly changing environment.

To the manager actually engaged in such activities, these changing waves of fashion seem somewhat unreal. The practitioner recognises that different problems require different methods of attack, and that the problems faced change over the course of time; but he or she also knows that such factors as the type of industry one is working in and the peculiar conditions of his or her particular firm are more important in determining the most appropriate approach to strategic planning and decision-making than differences in economic conditions between different decades. It is much more useful to regard these different approaches or emphases as providing a battery of weapons for attacking different types of problems, than as a series of continually improving products, each superseding the last and each uniquely appropriate to the needs of the time.[2]

The Diversity of Strategic Problems

The factors determining the nature of the strategic problems facing a particular enterprise may be divided into four groups:

1 the nature of the industry;
2 the nature of the enterprise;
3 the current circumstances of the firm;
4 the type of economy in which it is operating.

These are discussed in turn below.

The Nature of the Industry

The predominant strategic issues facing a firm to a large extent reflect the nature of the industry in which it is operating. Key factors are the type of products produced and markets served, the technology of production, and in some cases the nature of the materials required.

With some types of **product**, the development of new products or the introduction of new models may be the critical issues around which the determination of strategy revolves. The development of new products may require expensive investment in research and development, as with pharmaceutical products or aircraft; or it may be primarily a matter of market development and advertising, as with cosmetics. In either case, the strategic decisions whether to go ahead with the development of particular products may be the vital ones for the future of the company. At the other extreme, some products (e.g. metals or electricity) leave little scope for development.

Closely related to the type of product is the type of **market**. Commodity-type markets for standard products may leave little scope for strategic initiatives in marketing. If, however, a firm's products are 'differentiated' (that is, they have different and distinguishable characteristics from their competitors'), decisions about product design and markets become an important element in strategy. A new product may in itself create a new type of market that did not previously exist, as for example, the development of personal computers.

The greater the concentration of markets into the hands of a few major firms (as with the motor industry), the greater the need to consider the reactions of competitors to any strategic initiative. At the extreme, if a firm has a monopoly, or near monopoly, its strategy may revolve around how to maintain this position by keeping out new entrants.

The **technology of production** affects strategic issues in a variety of ways. In capital-intensive industries (like steel and chemicals) strategic planning tends to revolve around plant requirements and is frequently dominated by decisions about investment in new capacity (or closures). In labour-intensive industries, on the other hand, manpower policy may be more important – on the railways, for example. Assembly industries (like the motor industry) are concerned both with manning and component supplies. Integrated process industries may be more concerned with materials.

Finally, ensuring **access to materials** may be a major strategic concern, particularly in extractive industries such as oil, gas, coal, iron ore, etc. Mining and drilling rights and the accumulation of unexploited reserves may be vital to the firm's strategic future. Large firms in such industries tend to be multinationals, with strategic thinking heavily influenced by political factors.

Every type of industry has its own distinctive and diverse strategic problems: consider computer software, banking and horse-breeding, to name but three. A true appreciation of the nature and problems of the industry itself is an essential prerequisite for any successful strategy, and it is very difficult for any manager without this background to formulate an appropriate strategy for the firm.

The Nature of the Enterprise

The **size** of the firm affects both the nature of its strategic problems and the way they are tackled. The need for a generally agreed strategy is often more apparent in large firms than in small ones because of the complexity and diversity of their activities. Large firms also have greater resources to devote to the determination of strategy — more top management and more staff support. It is natural, therefore, that a great deal of the study of strategy and strategic planning techniques should have been directed at large corporations. But strategy can be equally important in small and medium-sized firms, particularly when they are at a turning point in their affairs — when the original management nears retirement, for example.

Ownership is another important influence. In the case of a small family-owned firm, personal aims are closely intertwined with those of the enterprise. The owner may not wish to expand the firm beyond the point where he can manage it himself; or on the other hand, he may be keen for it to reach a size where there is scope for other members of the family to join him.

Where the shares of a company are publicly held, strategy may still be dominated by one major shareholder and personal factors may then be an important influence. For example, the major shareholder may have a passionate desire to own a national newspaper quite unrelated to any return on such an investment. Again, where a major shareholder is a customer or supplier (e.g. in a part-owned subsidiary supplying components) his interests will be a vital influence on strategy.

In large companies, the shareholding is generally diffused widely and individual shareholders will exercise no direct influence on strategy, unless the company runs into difficulties and institutional investors become active. The management is thus for the most part free to follow its own particular strategy. But in doing so it will need to maintain investor confidence and ensure adequate dividend growth in order to keep the stock market happy and its share price at a level that will avoid take-over bids. Hence the freedom of management to determine strategy is constrained by the need to carry conviction in the stock market and keep predators at bay.

If the enterprise is state-owned, its strategy will be subject to a number of additional constraints. If it is a public corporation, the scope of its activities will probably be laid down by law, and it may be subject to various statutory obligations. It will have to pay particular attention to public pressures of various kinds, from trade unions, local authorities and other public bodies. Its finances will in most cases be subject to tight government control, and its strategy will inevitably be the concern of both the management of the enterprise and the government.

On the other hand, private ownership or privatisation, is not a guarantee that a public utility can operate with a free hand. The survival of such organisations as private sector companies depends on their ability to achieve and maintain public confidence. Moreover, the reactions of the relevant regulating body to any policy they adopt must be a major concern in formulating strategy.

The degree of **maturity** of the enterprise is also a significant factor. At the start, strategy must be concerned with the firm's initial objectives for establishing its activities and the means of doing so. After a period of successful operation, however, its initial momentum may run out and it may reach the critical stage of asking, 'Where should we go next?' The answer may well determine the long-term success or failure of the firm to build itself up into a major company. Later still in its life the firm may enter another critical phase when demand for its original product flattens out or starts to decline and it faces such questions as to whether to retrench or diversify.

A further feature affecting the strategic problems of an enterprise is the extent to which its activities are **national or international**. As soon as a predominantly national company begins to engage in overseas activities, its strategic problems become one degree more complex; and a genuine multinational with substantial activities in a number of different countries will face major strategic issues as to which countries to produce and sell in, as well as the usual run of issues affecting a large company in its industry.

Last, but not least, there is the distinction between (a) **single-industry companies** and (b) **conglomerates**, producing and selling a range of largely unrelated products. In practice, there is a spectrum, with these two types at the extremes and companies with various degrees of diversification of products in between. The degree of diversification, particularly in large companies, has a major impact both on their organisation and on their approach to strategic planning. (In terms of organisation, the large 'integrated' company producing related products in related production facilities will have some form of divisional organisation; the conglomerate is more likely to be organised into a holding company and subsidiaries.) In the extreme case the conglomerate is buying and selling enterprises with little positive impact on their management: it verges on the purely financial institution holding a portfolio of investments, but with the important difference that it controls the companies it owns and can replace their management and direct their strategy. This type of organisation calls for an approach to overall strategy which puts particular emphasis on decisions about the types of activity and product in which it is engaged; it may also require particular attention to dividend growth in order to achieve a favourable stock market reaction.

On the other hand, in the case of large integrated companies like airlines, steel companies and oil companies, whose different activities are closely interrelated, strategic decisions tend to be concerned more with the volume of sales and capacity, investment in new plant and research and development. Strategy in such concerns is more closely bound up with planning the human and physical means of achieving their objectives.

Current Circumstances

In approaching strategy it is thus essential first to consider how the nature of the firm and the nature of the industry affect the key strategic issues; but in addition, the particular circumstances of both the firm and the economy in which it is operating at the time will be major factors. Strategy in the middle of a depression takes on a very different aspect from strategy in a period of economic expansion. A depression may well bring financial difficulties, pressure for retrenchment and closures, and hence a much shorter planning horizon than when a firm is investing for expansion. This was a noticeable feature of the early 1980s. Strategy in an industry in crisis tends to be much more short-term than in one that is thriving, such as banking. A firm making heavy losses is dominated by the need to get back into the black; a firm with surplus liquidity or a strong financial base can cast around for suitable new fields to conquer. The trouble with books on business strategy (no doubt, this one included) is that, like their military counterparts, they tend to be concerned with refighting the last war. Full justice will probably not be done to the strategic problems of the post oil-shock period of the 1970s and 1980s with its high unemployment and high inflation rates until we have emerged from it.

Type of Economy

Finally, too little attention tends to be paid to the fact that different approaches to strategy are needed in different types of economy. Because so much of the writing on business strategy has been based on the experience and characteristics of the American economy, there is a tendency to take industrialised economies as the norm. But in developing countries less can be taken for granted. Supplies of components, industrial and social infrastructure and skilled manpower may not be available on demand as they are in more advanced economies. Government policy may be more important, either in terms of positive support — tariffs or the operation of import controls may be a crucial factor — or in terms of restrictive policies controlling investment. Developing countries frequently have a greater element of government planning and control and are less market-orientated than industrialised economies; this too influences the nature of strategic decisions and planning. So do differences in culture between different industrialised or developing countries. The expansion of American-owned hotel chains into Communist China raises interesting questions in this respect. If business strategy is to be of relevance to managers working in vastly different types of economies and culture, it must grow beyond the dominant concerns of the large American corporation into a wider environment.

Defining Strategy

Recent writers have produced a variety of definitions of business 'strategy', reflecting in some cases significantly differing approaches to the subject; and the question of definition is worthy of some attention for this reason alone.

Although strategic decisions are by definition of such importance that they affect the future of the organisation as a whole, they may be primarily concerned with particular dimensions or aspects of the business. For example, the postwar decision of Marks and Spencer to enter food retailing, and the more recent decision to sell furniture and furnishings, were concerned with their product range. Their other major initiatives such as opening a store in Paris, or buying Brooks Brothers in the US, were concerned with their geographical market. Such decisions about products and markets (the so-called 'product/market mix') are clearly very important, and for a long time they tended to dominate the attention of students of business strategy. Ansoff, the doyen of strategic writers, treats strategy as almost exclusively concerned with the relationship between the firm and its environment and hence with the selection of the products it produces and the markets it sells them in.[3]

There are, however, other potentially important areas of strategic concern. For example, there was British Leyland's strategic decision to link up with Honda; not only was this decision concerned with product/market mix, but it also had major implications for production and development policy (such as the use of Japanese components and know-how, and buying in a fully developed design). The whole of BL's future production and model development strategies was thrown open by the move.

Again, in the 1970s a major strategic issue facing the

British Steel Corporation was that of adapting to a new steelmaking technology and replacing open hearth by oxygen steelmaking (BOS). This involved the replacement of over thirty open hearth plants scattered over the country by five major BOS plants in the main steelmaking centres – a process of rationalisation which involved major reductions in manpower and acute social problems in a number of areas highly dependent on steel employment. This is a good example of a strategic decision primarily concerned with production technology.

An extreme example of a strategic issue which is wholly a production one without any product/market implications is the question of nuclear versus conventional power; this, and the choice of reactor system, is the major strategic issue facing many major electricity producers.

Consideration of the range of issues which should rightly be regarded as strategic, either from recent industrial experience or in a longer-term perspective, suggests a need for a wider definition. Chandler, in his 1962 study of the growth of the multi-divisional form of organisation in large American corporations in response to strategic change,[4] adopted a broader concept of strategy which covered the more diverse strategic issues that his historical studies revealed – for example, Standard Oil of New Jersey's search for new sources of oil to meet the insatiable appetite of the growing US market after the First World War. He defined strategy as 'the determination of the basic long-term goals and objectives of an enterprise, and the adoption of courses of action and the allocation of resources necessary for carrying out these goals'.

Ansoff and other writers in recent years have broadened the scope of what they regard as strategy to cover all aspects of the relationship between the firm and its environment, rather than just the product/market mix, and thus allow a greater variety of issues to be treated as strategic. For example, Hofer and Schendel, in one of the best books on strategy formulation, define strategy as 'the basic characteristics of the match an organisation achieves with its environment'.[5]

This approach provides scope for considering the supply aspects of a firm's relationship with its environment, but it fails to recognise explicitly major strategic issues that can arise within a firm, such as its manpower and production policies – for example, British Rail's and London Transport's struggle to economise on manpower in operating their railway systems or the safety problems involved.

Finally, a firm's strategy may be implicit rather than explicit, a point well made by Andrews (one of the earliest writers on the subject), whose comprehensive definition is worth quoting in full. 'Corporate strategy is the *pattern of decisions* in a company that determines and reveals its objectives, purposes, or goals, produces the principal policies and plans for achieving those goals, and defines the range of business the company is to pursue, the kind of economic and human organisation it is, or intends to be, and the nature of the economic and non-economic contribution it intends to make to its shareholders, employees, customers and communities' (my emphasis).[6]

These questions of definition are not just of academic interest (in the derogatory sense of the word 'academic'), but can be of major practical importance in applying concepts and techniques to particular situations. American writers' emphasis on the product/market mix and the relation of the firm to its environment reflect the fact that for many years they were able to take for granted the adoption by American firms of the most efficient methods of production. This has never been universally true, and the emergence of Japan as technologically the most rapidly improving industrial nation may alter the balance of American concern. One of the features of rapid Japanese success in products like calculators, photocopiers and machine tools has been research and development programmes focused on both the development of new high-technology products *and* the techniques of mass-producing them for world markets at low cost.[7] In the UK, with its relatively poor record of industrial efficiency and productivity growth, the need to emphasise the importance of production strategy as well as market and product strategy should be obvious.

Formulating Strategy

The problem of formulating strategy can vary widely from case to case, but there are certain common elements or steps that are applicable in most instances. In the simplest terms, these may be reduced to a basic sequence of seven key steps.[8]

1 setting provisional objectives;
2 assessing the probable future environment;
3 assessing the situation of the firm;
4 formulating alternative strategies;
5 evaluating these alternatives;
6 deciding on the favoured strategy (including revised objectives);
7 drawing up the plans needed to implement it.

The objectives set initially can only be provisional, because until the measures needed to achieve them have been defined it is unclear whether these objectives are feasible — or necessarily desirable — when viewed against what may be involved in attaining them. Nevertheless, to start with a set of objectives gives the whole exercise point.

The next steps are to take stock of the situation of the firm and to consider how possible future changes in the external environment may affect it: then to formulate possible strategies for the future of the business, in particular how to use the potential of the firm to exploit new or unexploited market opportunities. Consideration of *alternative* strategies is an important part of the process. Reluctance to consider more than one possible course of action is probably the most pervasive weakness in strategic management, and a frequent means of perpetuating policies that have been overtaken by the changing course of events. This is often a consequence of the Chairman or Managing Director concerned initiating a strategy exercise as a means of elaborating, or getting acceptance within the organisation for, a conclusion he has already arrived at — with pressure on management time and the day-to-day demands of the business providing convincing excuses. Clearly, a balance has to be struck as to how wide a range of alternatives is examined and how frequently the existing strategy is questioned; but the fact remains that consideration of alternatives is ultimately the key to devising a successful, if not the best strategy.

The process of evaluating alternatives covers both financial evaluation, in the sense of trying to assess the relative profitability and other financial consequences of different strategies, and the less quantifiable aspects of how they might affect the position of the company. For example, a retrenchment programme might look very favourable in financial terms, but the longer-term implications for the management structure and industrial relations may also be important factors to take into account.

Having evaluated the alternatives, a decision must be made as to the strategy to be adopted and detailed plans must be drawn up as to how to implement it.

The distinction between a 'strategy' and a 'strategic plan' is not a rigid one; but a strategy will be a broad statement of objectives and means of achieving them and will not need too-frequent revision; while a strategic plan is a more detailed and quantified statement of means, which will cover a period of years and will generally be rolled forward and revised annually. Many firms will only undertake a major review of strategy at intervals of several years, but in most cases will have an annual planning exercise to make and revise plans within a given strategic framework. The relative emphasis on the broad strategy and the plan with detailed quantification will vary according to the type of organisation and industry.

Corporate versus Business Strategy

A guiding strategy is needed both for the firm as a whole and for its constituent parts. Strategy for the firm as a whole is sometimes referred to as 'corporate strategy', as distinct from strategies for individual businesses within a major corporation. These businesses may correspond to organisational entities such as subsidiaries of the main holding company or divisions of a multi-divisional company, or they may be conceptual units delineated solely for strategic planning purposes and not recognised in the formal organisation of the company; the latter are frequently called '*Strategic Business Units*' (SBUs).

Some approaches to strategy are most relevant to corporate strategy in the above sense, others to the formulation of strategy for individual businesses.

Plan of the Book

The remainder of the book discusses the major elements in the process just outlined. Chapter 2 considers the problem of setting **strategic objectives**. The process of **assessing the environment** (i.e., economic, political, social and technological developments) is discussed in chapter 3, and the process of **assessing the situation of the company** in chapter 4.

A major instrument of strategic change is the process of **diversification**, i.e., expansion into a wider range of products. Chapter 5 discusses some of the problems of diversification, in particular the relationships between new and existing businesses needed to make diversification successful.

Chapter 6, on **portfolio analysis**, is concerned with formulation of strategy at corporate level in firms with a diverse 'portfolio' of different businesses, and is thus particularly relevant to the central management of conglomerates.

Competitive strategy, which is discussed in chapter 7, is concerned with the firm's position and policy in relation to its competitors. It is relevant both to strategy at corporate level and to smaller business units producing specified products or serving particular markets.

The greater the degree of integration between different activities within the firm, the greater the emphasis likely to be placed on planning. Chapter 8 discusses **strategic planning**, and the key role of investment, whether in new capacity or the development of new processes, products or markets.

Financial evaluation of both strategic options and investment projects is an essential element in strategy formulation. This is discussed in chapter 9, together with some of the attendant problems of forecasting.

While many of the elements of business strategy are common to both the private and the public sector, **state enterprises and public utilities** do raise particular problems and these are discussed in chapter 10. By contrast the formulation of strategy in **small, high-technology firms** (chapter 11) is much less formalised but of equal importance to the future of the enterprise concerned. Finally, chapter 12 considers current and future trends in strategic thinking under the heading, '**People and Change**'.

Notes

1 Sir Basil Henry Liddell Hart, *Strategy: The Indirect Approach* (4th edn), 1967.
2 For a succinct summary of different approaches see Bernard Taylor, 'The State of the Art', in John Grieve Smith (ed.), *Strategic Planning in Nationalised Industries*, 1984 (reprinted in *Long Range Planning*, June 1984).
3 In his classic *Corporate Strategy*, Ansoff wrote: 'Strategic decisions are primarily concerned with external, rather than internal, problems of the firm and specifically with selection of the product-mix which the firm will produce and the markets to which it will sell' (H. Igor Ansoff, *Corporate Strategy,* 1965).
4 Alfred D. Chandler, Jr, *Strategy and Structure: Chapters in the History of the American Enterprise*, 1962.
5 Charles W. Hofer and Dan Schendel, *Strategy Formulation: Analytical Concepts*, 1978.
6 Kenneth R. Andrews, *The Concept of Corporate Strategy* (2nd edn), 1980.
7 John Prentice, 'Competing with Japanese Technology', and M. Stone, 'Competing with Japan – The Rules of the Game', both in *Long Range Planning*, April 1984.
8 For a number of more elaborate models see in particular George A. Steiner, *Strategic Planning – What Every Manager Must Know*, 1979, pp. 24, 25.

2
Strategic Objectives

Whose Objectives?

The question of setting objectives in a strategic context is a more complex one than it might appear at first sight. It is noteworthy that writers on management are much more prone to emphasise the importance of defining strategic objectives than are managers themselves. The outside observer feels that management's plans and decisions would often be more effective if they had considered more carefully the precise objectives they were trying to achieve. Decision-makers, on the other hand, know from experience that it is difficult enough to reach agreement on the policy to be followed without also having to reach agreement on the ultimate objectives being pursued.

When discussing objectives in industry, the first question to ask is: Whose objectives? In considering the objectives of an enterprise there are several parties involved, whose interests, and hence objectives, may differ widely. The three most obvious are the shareholders, the managers and the workers.

I use the old-fashioned term 'workers' rather than 'employees' deliberately, in order to underline the potential conflict with management. In firms of any size there is a spectrum of employees from top management to the shop floor, many of whom have both some managerial and some employee or worker interest − the managerial element being dominant at the top and the employee element at the bottom. In the middle, a departmental manager, for example, has an interest as an employee in his department not being shut down, with the probable loss of his job; but he may also have a managerial interest in shutting down sections within his own department in order to improve the efficiency of the unit for which he is responsible.

Shareholders' Interests

The interests and objectives of shareholders may vary. For example, some may be interested primarily in high dividends now, and others in rising share prices or future growth. In large public companies, shareholders with differing interests tend to invest in the type of company whose nature or management style makes it an investment of the type they require: the specialist unit trust fund is an extreme example of this approach. Thus in many cases the type of company influences the type of investor rather than vice versa. But in private companies, or public companies with major individual shareholdings, the reverse tends to be true: the particular interests of the shareholder will affect the type of objectives to be pursued. There may, of course, also be conflicts between groups of shareholders themselves, particularly if one group is actually engaged in management. For example, in a family firm the generation managing the company (and earning managerial salaries) may be particularly interested in growth and reinvestment of profits; whereas other members of the family, who are either not involved in management or are retired from active participation, may be more interested in high dividends.

A similar difference in attitude may arise in relation to risk. Again, in a widely held public company the shareholders will adjust to the public view of the company's sensitivity to risk. But where there are influential groups of shareholders (either individual or corporate), their attitude to risk is important in determining acceptable objectives.[1]

We have so far been assuming that the shareholders' objective is to maximise total returns from dividends and changes in share prices although with some differences in emphasis on the present benefits *vis-a-vis* future benefits and on attitudes to risk. But certain types of shareholder may have other dominating objectives. For example, one firm may have taken an interest in another in order to safeguard its supplies of materials or components, or to secure an outlet for its products. Even if such a shareholder does not have a controlling interest, his objectives and interests will impinge sharply on the formulation of strategic objectives. Where a company is held 50/50 by two other companies with differing interests, the formulation of strategy is particularly difficult. An example of this was the Round Oak Steel Works, which was jointly owned by the British Steel Corporation and Tube Investments; the latter was interested in it primarily as a supplier of materials, the former as an enterprise selling partly to Tube Investments and partly to other customers.

Finally, the state as a shareholder, either in a public company or a statutory state enterprise, will have a number of wider and often conflicting interests. As owner it will want to see high profits and dividends; from a narrow budgetary point of view, it will want to keep down the borrowing requirement; but as the representative of the consumers, it will also be interested in low prices or high standards of service.

Managerial Interests

The phenomenon of the managerially controlled corporation has been around for over half a century. This has led to a great deal of discussion of managers' own objectives and the extent to which companies are not necessarily maximising profits; less attention has been paid to the way that the emphasis on professional management has reinforced the difference between the small businessman making money for himself and the manager of the large company making money for someone else. The divorce of ownership from control was first thoroughly documented in the classic study of the ownership of large American corporations by Berle and Means in the early thirties.[2] In his discussion of the implications of this for the 'technostructure' (i.e. the management of large corporations), Galbraith underlines the ironic fact that 'In the entrepreneurial corporation men at all levels work in principle at least, for the enrichment of someone else.'[3] Yet, curiously, both the manager and entrepreneur appear to subscribe to the same ethos. The artificiality of this is most striking when listening to the professional manager talking about the 'profit motive', without any acknowledgement of the difference between the profit motive in the sense of actually making money for oneself and the profit motive in the sense of showing better figures in the annual report.

Attempts to bridge this gap by share participation, bonus schemes and merit increases still leave the manager's individual prosperity and well-being depending much more on his position within the company than on the financial performance of the company. Nevertheless, one interest that managers generally have in common is the expansion of the company, and with it their spheres of command, as an avenue to promotion. Whether consciously or unconsciously, the objective of expansion, particularly for a manager's own part of the company's activities, bulks large in his concept of strategic objectives. So too does the protection of the interests of his own particular function or activity.

Nevertheless to go on to imply that there are inevitable conflicts between the managers' interest in expansion and the shareholders' interest in profitability (as do many of the so-called 'managerial theories of the firm') may be a false dichotomy, or at least an over-simplification.[4] The postulated conflict between expansion and profitability is based on the simplistic assumption that managers' drive for expansion is solely a matter of selling more of the same product in the same market at progressively lower prices, rather than widening the range of products sold and the markets served. It is amazing what an intellectual pack of cards has been erected on such a precarious assumption. Expansion and higher profits are generally necessary concomitants: it is only misconceived expansion that reduces profitability (i.e. creating over-capacity or diversifying into unsuitable products).

The more significant difference between shareholders and managers is their time horizon. Most holders of publicly quoted shares tend to take a very short-term financial view, and are mainly interested in the behaviour of the share price. Managers, on the other hand (like the more successful entrepreneurs) are generally concerned with the longer-term profitability and success of the firm.

Indeed one fundamental difference between the managers' objectives and those of the shareholders lies in their differing attitudes to the continued existence of the organisation. The manager tends to be heavily committed to the organisation which he has helped to create or run, and on whose existence his job depends, whereas the shareholder is perfectly prepared to see the organisation taken over or liquidated if it is financially advantageous to him to do so.

Employee Interests

Employee interests and objectives are more straightforward: high pay, good working conditions, job satisfaction and job security – not necessarily in that order. In so far as their experience and skills are not easily transferable, the employees have a deep interest in the long-term prosperity and survival of the firm.

There is frequently a significant divergence between the interests of different groups of employees. This is evident, for example, when there are proposals for closing down excess capacity but several plants that are alternative candidates for closure: the workers at each plant may then have diametrically opposed interests.

Where the issues at stake concern large numbers of employees and affect them in a similar manner, this collective interest can only be made effective in an organised manner by trade-union representation. There may, however, in particular circumstances be some divergence between trade union interests *per se* and the narrower interest of the employees of a particular firm. For example, the preservation of national bargaining may be important to the union but against the interests of the employees of one of the more prosperous firms in it.

Other Interests

There are also a number of other interests that come into play in determining strategic objectives. Most fundamental of these is the interest of the *customer*, since without a market the firm has no future.

In many cases the interests of the *suppliers* also have to be taken into account. For example, a motor manufacturer who is highly dependent on a variety of component suppliers would be ill-advised to formulate a strategy without considering their survival and well-being.

Another set of interested parties is the *banks and debtholders*, particularly if the firm is in financial difficulties. Any strategy formulated in these circumstances will have to have their interests well to the fore.

Then there is the *government*, central and local, and any other public bodies concerned with the firm or industry: their interests and concerns must be kept in view. Large firms in politically sensitive industries, like airlines or aerospace firms, are very sensitive to government action and regulation.

More loosely related to the firm, but still important, are the public *pressure groups*, whether highly organised like the environmental groups or arising *ad hoc* in response to local circumstances. Firms operating in a single locality, particularly where they are the major source of employment, are inevitably particularly sensitive to pressure from local interests.

Recognition of the variety of different groups or organisations that may have an interest in the conduct of the enterprise has led to what is called the 'Stakeholder Approach'. This suggests that the enterprise should be thought of as being run for the benefit of all these interested parties, and thus broadens the possible range of objectives of the enterprise to include those of the various stakeholders. The adoption of such an approach means that the formulation of objectives is complicated by the fact that different 'stakeholders' will have different, and often conflicting, objectives; or, in so far as they have common lists of objectives, the weight they each attach to different elements may differ markedly. For example, both management and workers may subscribe to higher labour productivity as an objective; but, in so far as it involves changes in established working practices and possible redundancies, workers may be far less anxious to pursue the objective than management. Lists of objectives may comprise a number of good things, but they will seem better to some parties than to others.

Weighing Different Objectives

The weight attached to the objectives of different groups and individuals depends on three main factors: the constitution and ownership of the organisation; the relative bargaining power of the groups; and the climate of public opinion.

The importance of the formal constitution is most evident in the case of statutory enterprises, where the powers, duties and composition of the managing board are prescribed by legislation, as are also the powers of the government or other regulatory body over the enterprise. The imposition of a statutory duty to consult trade-union and consumer representations may also strengthen the position of these interests (see chapter 10 for a discussion of the particular problems of state enterprises).

In the case of enterprises formed as public limited companies under UK and similar legislation, the formal constitution of the enterprise has, on the other hand, proved a remarkably loose constraint. The public company has turned out to be an extremely flexible organisation, capable of operating with widely differing distributions of power among the three main contenders: shareholders, management and workers. Although formally the shareholders and their representatives are the sole governing power, the absence of any statutory prescription of the rights and duties of executive management and workers or trade unions has fortuitously left a good deal of room for the evolution of a variety of different situations.

On the other hand, the fact that the legal framework of the company has not caught up with changes in the prevailing ethos, particularly in respect of employees' interests, can lead to a marked dichotomy between the legal position and what might be regarded as legitimate interests to be considered. A striking expression of this came in a letter to *The Times* from a general manager in a company involved in a take-over battle:[5]

> How can it be right that employees, such as myself, who are chained to the company by the pension rights that our years of service have

earned, should have no voice in a process under which our skills and talents, our enthusiasm and loyalty, are sold as property rights to whoever blindly pays the most?. . . it is a legal anachronism that the shareholders of a great company employing thousands of staff. . . should be entitled to sell the company without any form of consultation with management, customers or staff.

The take-over situation is, however, to some extent the exception that proves the rule; in the day-to-day operation of the business and in the formulation of longer-term strategy, the interests of management and other employees can rarely be ignored to this extent. Nevertheless, a key issue remains concerning the representation of employees in the formal structure of the company (as in the case of large companies in Germany) – in particular, whether they should be entitled as of right to representation on company boards, the practicalities of which in a UK context were explored in detail by the Bullock Committee in 1977.[6] Such representation would increase the relative power of the workers in the organisation and would influence its strategic objectives; so too would the parallel proposal that major companies should be formally obliged to consult their employees about their strategic plans. Such representation has been obligatory in German coal and steel companies for many years and has now been extended to other large companies. While such measures went out of favour in the UK during the Thatcher era, they have received a new impetus in the European Community in the context of the discussion of a European Charter of Social Rights.

Social Objectives

The most difficult group of objectives to put into perspective are those that are generally termed 'social', i.e. as opposed to 'economic' costs or benefits that do not readily bear a price tag. These tend to fall into two categories: (a) those affecting the people connected with the enterprise, such as the quality of life within the organisation, job security, occupational health hazards and discrimination by sex, race or religion and (b) social factors external to the organisation, such as pollution, the effect of the company on the local community or the effect of the products on the consumer (e.g. tobacco). The increasing concern of top management in large American firms with political and social factors is recorded in George A. Steiner's study of the 'The New Class of Chief Executive Officer', based on interviews with 47 top managers in very large American corporations.

> There is no question at all about the fact that CEOs of the largest corporations have formulated a strategy to be responsive to the non-economic as well as the economic forces operating in their environment...Today's CEOs believe that a strong and viable business system will not exist in a society where a majority of the public perceives the private interests of people in business as being opposed to public interests. Top managers of our corporation believe, and rightly so, that the corporation is and should be fundamentally an economic institution...But they go beyond that. They believe that as corporations grow larger social programs which they undertake voluntarily become more necessary and important...They realise that there is, however, a limit to what they can and should be doing in the social area...Nevertheless the philosophical difference between their accepting voluntarily constituent pressures to pursue social programs and their denying that they have any obligations to do so is very great and important.[7]

This is a more realistic and balanced statement of the case than some, which tend to suggest that economic objectives have actually been supplanted by social or political objectives.

There has been some movement recently among a minority of large companies in the UK towards developing social responsibility programmes, in particular in inner-city areas, and assisting in the development of small businesses. The latter, in particular, has the advantage of mobilising existing industrial skills where they may be urgently needed.

Without wanting to decry such activities, it must nevertheless remain true that the basic objectives of the enterprise, whether privately or state-owned, must be industrial. Management may be constrained by law, by social pressures or by the prevailing ethos to satisfy certain social obligations – such as not to discriminate by race or sex, or to keep pollution within certain limits. But is is misleading to treat the abolition of discrimination or the minimisation of pollution as primary objectives of the firm. There have been occasional entrepreneurs for whom social objectives of this type have been as important as economic objectives: Robert Owen, the Cadbury family and Wilfred Brown of Glacier Metal, for example – but they are few and far between. Most businessmen or managers, whether in the private or public sector, are primarily concerned with industrial objectives, and fulfil such social obligations which cost money (such as limiting pollution) only to the extent required by legal, social or moral pressures, the prevailing ethos within the firm and their own sense of morality.

Objectives and Constraints

In practice, firms are run primarily for the benefit of the three parties mainly concerned: shareholders, management and employees. The interests of other parties represent a constraint rather than an objective. In other words, they are something to be satisfied up to a certain level rather than maximised.

Even among the three main parties, the distinction between what is an objective and what is a constraint depends on the party in question. For the shareholders, maximum profits will be an objective and an adequate or good level of wages a constraint. On the other hand, for the employees, adequate dividends to satisfy the shareholders will be a constraint, and as high a level of pay as possible an objective. Both points of view are legitimate.

Hierarchy of Objectives

Strategic objectives may be regarded as forming a hierarchy with the most general purposes of the enterprise at the top descending through more precise objectives (e.g. financial targets) for the organisation as a whole down to objectives for particular activities or functions. The potential conflict of interest between various groups may manifest itself at all these levels.

General Purposes

The idea that a firm should have a formal statement of its general purposes or *mission* is more popular in America and Japan than in Great Britain, where most firms do not feel such a need. Such statements can take two basic forms. One is more of a creed, or statement of beliefs, with an emphasis on values and all the different worthwhile objectives that the company is aiming at. The trouble with this sort of statement is twofold. First, it is frequently regarded as a pious public relations exercise viewed with some cynicism by those within the company — even where it does in part reflect the ethos of the firm. Second, listing a series of objectives, each good in itself (e.g. high quality, efficient production, high wages, low costs), is valueless without some consideration of the weight to be attached to each when there is some potential conflict or trade-off between them; they cannot all be maximised simultaneously.

More valuable is the statement of business purpose, which represents in effect a statement of strategy at the highest level of generality and serves both as an effective guide in the strategic conduct of the business and as a bond in giving the employees a common feeling of purpose.

One of the conclusions that comes through most clearly from Peters's and Waterman's best-selling study of a group of successful American firms, *In Search of Excellence*, is that they virtually all had 'a well-defined set of guiding beliefs', culture or even mythology.[8] 'Everyone at Hewlett-Packard knows that he or she is supposed to be innovative.' 'Everyone at Proctor and Gamble knows that product quality is the sine qua non.' Similar statements of purpose seem particularly to fit the culture of the Japanese firm, with its emphasis on co-operative activity to achieve a common goal. They seem to have taken least root in British conditions, where those working in an enterprise may value their right to differ about values and general objectives provided they can agree on specific decisions and policies, particularly where the inheritance of the class system and the ideology of most trade-union activists create a strong divide between managers and workers. Nevertheless, the success of certain Japanese firms in starting subsidiaries in the UK suggests that such statements, properly handled, may not be as alien as they might at first sight appear – after all, the 'team spirit' has quite an indigenous ring.

Statements of general purpose would seem most meaningful in organisations founded and dominated by one person, one family or a small group with common aspirations: Sainsbury's and Marks and Spencer, for example. They seem least likely to be meaningful in large organisations run by shifting coalitions of different interests. This applies particularly to public bodies such as nationalised industries, with various potentially conflicting interest groups represented on the board.

Strategic Objectives

The second step down the hierarchical ladder represents strategic objectives: that is, broad objectives directed at the long-term profitability and survival of the enterprise, such as developing a comprehensive model range, diversifying into related activities or starting manufacturing activities in other countries. These long-term objectives may be changed from time to time, but they remain valid for long enough to be achieved and are certainly not subject to annual revision.

Corporate strategic objectives are either comprehensive enough or critical enough to affect the whole organisation. The achievement of such objectives may in turn call for a subsidiary set of objectives for different parts of the organisation: subsidiaries, divisions, or strategic business units. (Whereas subsidiaries of holding companies, and divisions of multi-divisional organisations are distinct organisational units, the term 'strategic business unit' is frequently used to denote an area of the business that is a significant entity for strategic planning purposes but not organisationally separate for operational purposes.) This set of subsidiary objectives will cover the whole range of possible developments of individual businesses and mirror on a smaller scale the type of strategic objectives set for the organisation as a whole. Objectives may also be set for different functions (either at corporate or lower levels). This will comprise such things as sales targets, industrial relations objectives, manpower reductions, etc. At the end of the day, the strategic plan for the company as a whole must comprise a series of objectives to guide all its various divisions and departments.

Finally, it should be emphasised that the task of balancing conflicting objectives is a fundamental feature of all forms of managerial decision-making. At the strategic level, apart from conflicts in objectives arising from conflicts in interests between stakeholders, there is also potential conflict between short- and long-term objectives (for example between cutting overheads and maintaining expenditure on research and development) or between parallel objectives (e.g., keeping down costs by rationalising the product line, or continuing to produce existing products to keep customers happy). The fact that such conflicts can be resolved in more than one way is one that disciplines such as economics and operational research have been reluctant to acknowledge; because they tend to assume that the effects on profits of pursuing these objectives can be estimated precisely and thus the single goal of profit maximisation over time can subsume all other more limited objectives. In the real world, however, the difficulty in quantifying or forecasting the effects of such factors leaves the concept of optimisation as purely theoretical, and the manager is left to use his judgement to balance up a multiplicity of (at least partly) conflicting objectives. This is particularly true at the strategic level.

Setting Financial Objectives

Financial objectives are naturally of fundamental importance to business organisations, whether as an end in themselves, as a measure of success or as a necessary condition for survival.

The most common type of financial objective is to achieve a

specified profit by a certain date, either in absolute terms or as a rate of return on capital. Financial objectives may, however, not be set wholly in terms of the growth in profits. A certain level for the debt/equity ratio may itself be an objective. The profit target may also be a means of achieving a target for dividend growth and share price; and there may be a related objective for the build-up (or investment of) reserves.

Any target for return on capital must take into account:

1 capital employed;
2 capital structure;
3 vintage of plant;
4 inflation.

The most basic measure of the adequacy of the profits is the return on investment at *replacement cost*. Unless the return is evaluated against replacement cost, it is highly dependent on the rate of inflation since the original investment was made. Profits in relation to the historical cost of the plant will rise with inflation; hence the return on book value at historical cost tends to rise and give an over-optimistic view of the real profitability of the operation — which may be one reason why inflation accounting has never become popular!

A firm's attitude to both the level of return and the degree of risk involved will depend on its capital structure, i.e. the proportion of total capital represented by (a) debt and (b) equity, in the form of either share capital or reserves. The higher the proportion of debt, the greater the danger of profits being insufficient to pay interest. While nobody wants to cut dividends, a high proportion of equity gives a greater safety margin in times of financial difficulty. The more the business has been financed by putting money into reserves, the less risk there is of defaulting on interest payments or cutting dividends. But the converse danger of self-financing is that it may involve accepting unduly low returns on the capital actually employed; the consequent undervaluation of the share capital by the market may invite take-over bids.

The 'vintage' of the plant can be an important factor in

setting appropriate profit targets in capital-intensive industries. Even in large companies, investment in plant and equipment is not evenly spread over the years; it tends to be bunched because of the timing of opportunities for expansion or technical changes. This might not matter if the profit-earning capacity of the plant followed the profile of the written-down book-value; but if the value is written down more rapidly than profits deteriorate with age, the rate of return will tend to go up over the years. At the extreme, plant fully written off in the books may still be making a profit — and thus showing an infinite rate of return. This fact, albeit with the effects of inflation noted above, means that returns on the book-value of plant need to be treated with extreme care, and that to take a particular return on investment (ROI) as a primary strategic objective can be dangerously misleading.

In capital-intensive industries, new investment can often reduce the average return on investment both because of high returns on written-down plant and because of the effects of inflation. This may be one reason why capital-intensive industries often show a low rate of return. The larger the firm's individual investments, the more careful it needs to be about taking return on investment as a target. This may seem paradoxical, as return on investment is clearly of such fundamental importance. But the danger lies in picking arbitrary numbers for ROI targets. This danger is less marked in firms with a wide spread of assets investing steadily year by year, but even so, the effects of inflation and depreciation policy need watching carefully.

Profit targets cannot be both arbitrary and realistic. This applies even to the simple target of 'getting out of the red' when the firm is making a loss. Such targets must take into account the starting point (current results) and the potential for change. They must also be considered carefully in relation to the nature of the strategy, in that the target for future profits and the nature of the strategy to be pursued must be consistent. Consolidation or expansion will involve different profit profiles over the years in question. Above all, in setting profit targets, the most obvious point to remember is that, even if everything in the company's control were to go according to plan (and it never does), outside forces are bound to make the outcome uncertain.

Preliminary and Final Objectives

The process of setting objectives must be an iterative one. The first stage is to set preliminary objectives; the next is to consider the various possible means of achieving them. The feasibility of the original objective must then be considered in the light of these possibilities. This applies particularly to quantitative objectives such as profit or sales targets. Preliminary objectives 'plucked out of the air' sitting round the Chairman's coffee table may well not appear realistic after detailed study. It is vital at this point to substitute more realistic objectives. Similarly, if objectives set in the past no longer seem attainable in the light of subsequent events, they should be revised. This may at first sight seem faint-hearted, but it is very rare indeed for 'aiming at the impossible' to be a fruitful policy in a complex industrial situation. Plans designed to achieve unrealistic objectives become unrealistic throughout the organisation; they are then treated with cynicism, and effectively the organisation is reduced to operating without any plan at all. Alternatively, certain arbitrary sub-objectives may be maintained, although out-dated, at the expense of making the best of the situation as it actually is.

It is important to consider objectives before, during and at the end of any strategic planning exercise to ensure that they are realistic and that the problem of striking a balance between conflicting objectives has been properly evaluated. For example, setting an objective of expanding sales volume by 10 per cent is arbitrary without an examination of the extent to which orders can be batched together to give longer production runs, the costs involved etc.

Gap Analysis

The concept of a 'strategic gap' between the objective sought and the likelihood of achieving it is a simple, but very useful, analytical tool. If, for example, the strategic objective is to achieve a certain level of profits in five years' time, the analysis would start with a forecast of profits in that year on the assumption of a continuation of existing policies. This forecast is then compared with the profit objective, and the difference represents the strategic gap to be filled if the objective is to be achieved (see figure 2.1).

The next step is to consider the various steps that might be taken to close the gap, either as alternatives or in combination – in other words, to analyse the benefits to be obtained from different strategic moves. Consideration of such moves may provide a means of closing the gap, wholly or partially; in the latter case, either a strategic objective must be modified or more radical strategies must be sought.

This approach can be applied to the profitability of the organisation as a whole or parts of it, or to intermediate objectives such as sales targets. By starting from a forecast of the effects of continuing with present policies, it establishes the basic point that a 'neutral' policy of carrying on as before does not necessarily mean staying as profitable as today.

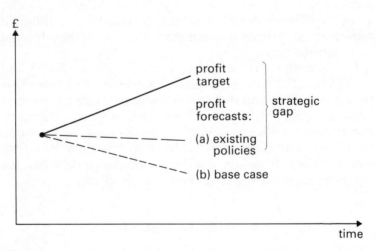

Figure 2.1   Strategic gap

It should be noted that the bottom line in the figure can take two forms. The first is a forecast on the basis of a continuation of existing policies, which could mean, for example, continuing heavy investment. The other is a 'base case', involving the minimum investment needed to keep the plant going. In more general terms, the first is 'carrying on as before'; the second is doing the minimum. When considering strategies involving investment, it is important to look at the 'base case' as well as the 'continuation of existing policies' in order to avoid assuming that continued substantial investment is necessarily inevitable. We shall return to this point in chapter 9 on investment.

Notes

1 For a stimulating discussion of this point see John Argenti, *Systematic Corporate Planning*, 1974, chapter 3.
2 Adolf A. Berle and Gardiner C. Means, *The Modern Corporation and Private Property*, 1932.
3 John Kenneth Galbraith, *The New Industrial State*, 1967.
4 For a discussion of managerial theories of the firm see Donald A. Hay and Derek J. Morris, *Industrial Economics, Theory and Evidence*, 1979, chapters 8 and 9.
5 Mr R. C. Howroyd, *The Times*, 31 December 1983.
6 *Report of the Committee of Inquiry on Industrial Democracy* ('Bullock Committee'), January 1977. This Committee was set up by the Labour government largely in response to pressure from the Trades Union Congress.
7 George A. Steiner, 'The New Class of Chief Executive Officer', *Long Range Planning*, August 1981.
8 Thomas J. Peters and Robert H. Waterman, Jr, *In Search of Excellence*, 1982.

3

Assessing the Environment

While strategy should not be conceived as exclusively concerned with the relation between the enterprise and its environment, assessing the effects of possible future changes in the environment is an essential task in formulating strategy. (We use the term 'environment' here to cover all factors external to the firm, not in the limited sense of physical environment used when talking about pollution, etc.)

There are two steps to this process: the first is to consider how the relevant environmental factors may change; the second is to assess the strategic implications of such changes for the firm. These are here considered in turn.

Changes in Environmental Factors

Environmental factors may be classified under four main headings:

1 economic;
2 social and demographic;
3 political;
4 technological.

Economic Factors

Economic factors comprise both the general development of the national and world economies and also developments specific to the industry or enterprise in question. The general economic climate is a major factor, affecting the prosperity of large and small businesses alike, but one whose significance is often underrated. When the sales of a commodity are depressed, for example, there is frequently a tendency to search for special factors to account for the loss of sales, when it is really only a consequence of a general contraction in consumer spending. Firms will be affected not only by the general level of demand in the economy, but also by particular financial factors such as exchange rates, interest rates, etc. Thus, macroeconomic developments are a vital external force on all businesses but are also extremely difficult to forecast in the longer run.

Consider for a moment the succession of drastic changes that the world economy has gone through in the last 60 years. The first of these started with the 1929 financial crisis and subsequent slump. This was a period of heavy unemployment in North America and Europe which lasted up to the start of the Second World War in 1939. The main mitigating factor was the onset of rearmament.

The Second World War saw the emergence of controlled economies and full employment in the United Kingdom and the United States, but ended with physical devastation across much of Europe. The initial postwar years were devoted to physical reconstruction in Europe and the conversion of wartime to peacetime economies. This period of reconstruction gave way to one of growth in the late 1950s and 1960s. Employment remained high but there was growing concern about rising prices. After a spell of what might be regarded as some sort of 'normality', the oil crisis in the early 1970s was followed by a period of slow growth, rising unemployment and spiralling prices.

Inflation eased and unemployment peaked in most industrial countries by the mid 1980s; but unemployment remained high by postwar standards and the era of full employment seemed to have come to an end. The imbalance in trade between the OPEC and industrialised countries was replaced by major imbalances between industrialised countries, with the US balance of payments in massive deficit in the second half of the 1980s and Japan and Germany with growing surpluses. A new period of exchange rate instability had begun.

This bare catalogue of developments over the last 60 years shows that drastic change is not a new occurrence that suddenly emerged with the oil crisis. It also makes the point that the most successful period of economic development in terms of growth and employment was the 1950s and 1960s.

It is not merely conditions that change but the way in which the world economy works or the relations between the key variables. For example, the accepted theoretical and practical wisdom about the sustainability of balance of payments deficits and their effect on exchange rates failed to explain the behaviour of the dollar in the late 1980s. The growing international mobility of investment funds meant that favourable capital movements could finance a US balance of payments deficit on a scale hitherto unsuspected, as long as US interest rates and stock market conditions were attractive to the outside world. The planning assumption that the deficit would be unsustainable and the dollar must inevitably decline drastically proved only partially true.

What then can we expect in the 1990s? Will the trade imbalance between the US, on the one hand, and Germany and Japan on the other, persist − or if it starts to be resolved will the mechanism of change be exchange rate adjustments or trade policy? Will the developing countries' debt problems continue to simmer indefinitely? Will the industrialised countries continue to operate at relatively high levels of unemployment without a political backlash? Will political change open up vast new areas of trade with Russia and Eastern Europe? What will be the consequences of *rapprochement* between Russia and China?

These are typical of the key uncertainties facing anyone trying to assess the economic outlook. There are in effect two levels of economic forecasting. The first, which is difficult enough, is to forecast developments on the assumption that we continue broadly within the same phase or type of situation − the typical quantitative forecast put out by regular forecasting bodies. The second, and more difficult, is to consider the possibility of major changes or 'discontinuities' in basic economic conditions and the relations between key variables.

It is unrealistic to expect staff in any one firm to get the right answers when external forecasters in government or research institutes with greater resources cannot do so. (Indeed, the fact that many professional forecasters failed to spot crucial turning points has made them reluctant to step out of line. Here as elsewhere there is safety in numbers, and if the company economist can show that his forecasts are well within the band displayed by the leading institutes in this field, he feels he has at least safeguarded himself against charges of professional incompetence.) The main requirement is that management should appreciate the possibility of major changes in the economic environment in which they have to operate, and consider the possible effects of changes which might be particularly significant to their company.

Social and Political Factors

Changing social customs may be an important factor influencing the nature and size of the market for particular products. For example, even the traditional British 'pub' has been transformed in recent years: the increasing number of women customers has affected the pattern of drink sold and the standard of comfort acceptable; and the trend towards eating out has made food sales as important as drink. The new market for package holidays in the sun has developed at the expense of the old-fashioned British seaside holiday. Again, changes in social attitudes may affect the way in which organisations operate. For example, the dictatorial style of management is becoming less and less acceptable.

Attitudes to the large industrial corporation have remained (in shifting proportions) a mixture of criticism and resignation for the last 50 or more years. In Britain the debate has concentrated on the question of public ownership, and by the end of the 1980s the pendulum had swung to extremes of privatisation. In the United States much of the discussion in principle has been concerned with the relation between management and shareholders, and the extent to which social or other objectives should temper the pursuit of profit;[1] but the main issue in practice has been the thrust of anti-trust regulation − an area where judgement of the climate of opinion and administrative practice may be of crucial importance.

Social change in most countries is very slow – frustratingly slow for those who are trying to secure such changes: for example, changes in attitudes towards the role of women in industry. It appears to be rather less slow in the United States than elsewhere, however, which may be one reason why American writers may appear to British eyes to over-emphasise the effects of social change.

Political change can be an important factor for businesses of all kinds. First, changes in government policy towards industry as a whole may affect firms in a variety of ways: through taxation, exchange controls, public ownership, legislation affecting employment, pollution control, etc. (the list is endless). In a democracy such changes seldom come unheralded by prior public discussion; the major uncertainty is generally the result of the next election. But a change in government may lead to major changes in attitude and approach.

Such changes can be even more sudden and drastic when they follow a revolution or *coup d'état* – the experience in Iran following the overthrow of the Shah and the assumption of power by the Islamic fundamentalist Ayatollah Khomeini was a spectacular example. Even so, the seeds of revolution have often been sown many years beforehand. Now equally revolutionary changes are taking place in Eastern Europe and Russia with political liberalisation and the failure of the 'command economy'. China seems likely to follow suit sooner or later.

Particularly in democracies, political and social attitudes are subject to short-term cycles as well as long-term trends. Attitudes to plant closures are a good example. In the 1970s large-scale plant closures were regarded in the UK and elsewhere as major social disasters, to be avoided if at all possible. The strategies of many large firms in Germany and elsewhere included among their objectives the main-tenance of overall employment, and the replacement of old products with newer ones, if possible in the same or nearby locations.

In the 1980s the pendulum swung the other way. Recession made closures commonplace. In the UK the Thatcher government placed greater emphasis on profitability and industrial efficiency and less on social factors. Nevertheless, the longer-term trend towards giving greater weight to the social factors inhibiting closures seems likely to re-emerge as and when business conditions generally improve.

A similar cycle has been evident in the UK attitudes to trade-union participation in management, partly associated with changes in government and partly with changes in the predominant public attitude towards the trade unions. The movement in favour of trade-union representation on company boards reached its peak in 1977 with the report of the Bullock Committee on Industrial Democracy, set up to discuss methods of implementing such proposals. The election of the Conservative government in 1979 halted any move in this direction for the time being, but the development of common European social policies has revived the whole question of trade-union participation in both strategy formation and day-to-day management. Long-term consideration of an enterprise's labour relations strategy must take this into account.

Technological Factors

Technological change can affect a firm in two main ways: it may provide it with the opportunity to produce new products or adopt new processes; or it may alter the environment in which the firm operates, for example by leading to competition from new products, creating new markets or affecting the costs of supplies. The firm is thus concerned with technological development at two levels of intensity. The first is with developments within its own industry; the second is with developments elsewhere that impinge on it. These might be categorised as the 'active' and 'passive' aspects, except that changes in the business environment resulting from technological developments may provide profitable opportunities to exploit.

It is unusual for major technological developments to

appear suddenly without several years' warning that they are a possibility. The uncertainty about their success is most frequently economic rather than purely technical, in that the process or product is seen to be a technical possibility well before it is established whether or not it is likely to be economic. Hence a great deal of uncertainty about technological progress is specific. The nature of the potential threat or benefit is known: what is uncertain is whether it will emerge as a commercial reality.

Depending on the size of the firm and the extent of its research and development effort, forecasting technological change in its own industry will to a varying extent be a matter of forecasting how far the firm's own efforts will be successful and how far other people's will be. It is obviously important that a firm's strategy should take fully into account the potential of its own research and development effort and that, correspondingly, this effort should be integrated into the overall strategy. It is, however, quite common for this not to be the case in large companies if the research and development staff do not have an influential voice in the decision-making process. They may well be working on processes, which if developed successfully, would effectively destroy the company's existing strategy, because no consideration has been given to the need for a flexible strategy which facilitates the exploitation of these new processes or products.

An example of such an inconsistency was the British Steel Corporation's treatment of the possible development of the production of steel sheet from powder, which would have replaced existing hot strip mill technology. At one stage it became apparent that, although a considerable effort was being put into developing such technology, its successful development would have invalidated the enormous sums being put into investment in conventional technology, and no effort was being made to construct a strategy that would allow for the possible success of the new technology. Recognition of this led to the development of a strategy for stainless steel products which explicitly provided for a series of decisions to be made on the production of strip according to the success or otherwise of the pilot and prototype facilities then envisaged for this process. (A corresponding strategy for mild steel strip mill products proved more elusive, but expenditure on the alternative process fell victim to economy measures and the dilemma to some extent resolved itself.)

A key strategic decision in the case of new products or processes is whether to take the risks of being a leader or a follower in introducing them. The leader runs the danger of running into expensive teething troubles, but also stands to secure substantial gains through being ahead of competitors. The follower pursues a safer strategy: he may also gain through installing an improved Mark II process. A classic case is Matsushita who 'rarely originates a product but always succeeds in manufacturing it for less and marketing it best'.[2] While Sony pioneered the technology of video-tape recorders, Matsushita developed a more compact, longer playing system that took two-thirds of the market. In principle, the choice between being a leader or a follower should largely reflect the resources of the company in relation to the risk involved, but in practice it more often reflects the general tone and spirit of the company.

The intense concern with technological forecasting and uncertainty in management writing in recent years is very much a reflection of their almost exclusive attention to industrialised countries. In developing countries the situation is different, in that the main problem is to introduce known technology — not necessarily at the most advanced level — rather than to push forward the frontiers of technology. This is not to deny that there are in many developing countries a few leading firms who operate on technological standards that equal or approximate to world-best practice (e.g. shipbuilding in South Korea), but these tend to account for a very small section of the economy. Most firms in developing countries are concerned with strategic decisions about investment and product lines which are well within the boundaries of known technology in the industrialised countries. A key element in strategic choice is then to determine the economically and culturally appropriate technology in relation to the resources available to the company. (This choice may go by the board if international financial and plant manufacturing interests continue to offer the developing country virtually the same plant package on credit as they would install in those parts of the world with the highest labour costs.

Assessing the Impact of Change

The possible areas of environmental change that may affect a firm are inevitably very wide indeed, and even the largest organisations have not the time or resources to examine more than a fraction of the factors that might affect them. The more general the factors, the greater use that can be made of outside institutions and forecasting bodies – for example, for general economic forecasts. Even so, if such general developments are crucial to the firm, management is bound to consider the possibilities in some detail. The problem in environmental assessment or forecasting is to identify and concentrate on the areas of possible change which are most important to the organisation concerned.

There are two ways of tackling this. The first may be called the 'Outside-In' approach and the second, the 'Inside-Out'.[3] With the *'Outside-In' approach* you start by considering particular types of environmental change (say, the position of women in society) and then go on to consider all the various ways in which the organisation may be affected by such a change (markets, personnel, etc.). With the *'Inside-Out' approach* you start with the firm's various functions and products and consider in each case what environmental factors may be significant.

The former approach is obviously much more open-ended, and can be applied on only a limited scale. But where there are possible major changes that appear to deserve consideration (for example, an interruption of Middle East oil supplies) it is useful to start from the external factor and try to identify all its possible ramifications for the firm. This is, however, essentially a task for a central policy or planning staff, which is only likely to be available in a large company.

The second '*Inside-Out*' approach of starting from the firm's own functions and products is best suited to the organisation of most companies: the task of environmental analysis can initially be broken down between those departments engaged in the strategic review or planning exercise. The marketing department, for instance, will then be responsible for assessing potential market developments resulting from all the various environmental factors. The personnel department will be responsible for considering any future developments affecting the supply of manpower. The purchasing and transport departments will be responsible for considering future availability and costs of materials and transport etc.

In each case, the search is for changes in the environment which may significantly affect the company. It is important to beware of casting the net too widely and indiscriminately in a desire to examine every possible factor.

The concept of the environmental assessment as a search for environmental *threats* and *opportunities* has now become one of the handful of well-established and widely accepted ideas in the process of strategy formulation. It underlies the fundamental point that changes in markets or other external factors may constitute either a *threat to* an established business activity, or an *opportunity for* an extension of existing activities or the introduction of new activities or new methods. The categorisation of the potential effects of such changes into threats (bad) or opportunities (good) is, however, often a dangerous oversimplification. For example, the development of smaller computers constituted both a threat to the established large computer manufacturers, but also a potential opportunity for a vast expansion of their business. The challenge to the entrepreneur is to find a way of exploiting such change.

Environmental Assessment in Practice

In adopting the 'Inside-Out' approach to assessing the affect of possible environmental changes on the enterprise, it is convenient to examine the impact by four main areas:

1 market;
2 production and personnel;
3 fuel and material supplies;
4 finance.

Market

The impact of possible future change in the firm's sales depends on (a) the effect on the total market and (b) the firm's market share. The importance of general economic developments on demand has already been stressed. For many large companies, particularly those where there is little change in the nature of the product, macroeconomic developments will be the prime determinant of the general level of market demand. Hence their strategies will be highly dependent on the assumptions made about general economic developments. Whether they plan to expand will depend largely on their assessment of future development in the relevant economies as a whole. If demand for their products is depressed, the nature of the action they take will depend on their assessment of whether any economic recession is likely to be purely temporary or longer-lived.

The impact of other more specific factors varies immensely. To take three examples. First the demand for beer. General economic conditions, through their impact on personal disposable income, play a significant part. But in the longer run, changes in consumer habits and tastes are also important. In recent years there have been shifts in the pattern of drinking, both inside and outside the home. The increase in wine consumption is having a major impact on beer consumption. Drink/driving legislation has created a new market for low-alcohol lagers. Strategic thinking, in a major brewery company, must consider the impact of changing customs both on its licensed premises and on the pattern and level of its sales.

A different type of product, sold to both domestic and industrial consumers, is gas. The general level of economic activity will affect both industrial use and (via personal disposable incomes) domestic use. Other important determinants of demand in the longer term include changes in fuel efficiency, associated with the installation of more efficient equipment and appliances, and competition with other fuels (oil, coal and electricity). In formulating strategy for gas, the impact of possible changes in these influences on demand must all be carefully considered. So too must possible changes in supply conditions — for example in the United Kingdom, the limits and changing cost conditions for supplies of gas from the North Sea.

A third example, subject to quite different influences, is the funeral undertaking business. The number of funerals is presumably equal to the number of deaths, which is determined by demographic and health factors. How much is spent on each funeral, however, depends on factors such as: social customs, car ownership, prevalence of insurance and its adequacy in the face of inflation and preferences for cremation as compared with burial.

The reader can multiply examples. For instance, what are the main environmental factors likely to affect the market for after-shave lotions and other male toilet preparations over the next five years?

In assessing the prospects for market share, rather than the total market, it is necessary to consider possible changes in the competitive power of other firms selling in the same market — for example, the introduction of new or improved products, the installation of new productive capacity, and changes in strategy or tactics. One of the difficulties with market share is to distinguish targets from forecasts. If every firm in the industry is aiming to increase its market share, it cannot be realistic for them all to forecast success!

Production

The main instigator of change on the production side is likely to be technological developments. As suggested above, these are frequently more predictable in the medium term than tends to be assumed. New processes and techniques of major significance have a lead-time of some years from initial work in the laboratory to the installation and effective operation on a commercial scale. The uncertainty lies not so much in the nature of such developments, but in whether they will turn out to be economic and satisfactory in full-scale operation. Their competitive impact depends not only on their effects in reducing costs, but also very often on improvements in product quality. I remember being amazed by a factory manager who was showing me round a watch factory in India where dozens of women were assembling watches. He told me he was anxious to get the plant fully automated. Faced with my incredulity that this could be economic in the circumstances, he argued that only automation would enable them to compete internationally in terms of quality.

In the steel industry, continuous casting has been established for many years as a more economic production route for many products than ingot rolling. When the British Steel Corporation (BSC) was first considering the introduction of continuous casting for producing steel for tinplate, Metal Box, its major customer, was apprehensive that the new production would not be satisfactory, and had to be enticed into acceptance by promises that it would benefit from the consequent cost reductions. In the event, the installation of continuous casting at the South Wales works was delayed; Metal Box became increasingly impatient at its inability to obtain from BSC continuously cast material, which they now considered essential to provide the consistency of quality needed for high-speed can-making lines, and which they could obtain from American sources. The moral here is that the introduction of new processes involving an improved product has to be geared carefully to market developments. Early development requires intensive marketing to gain acceptance, and then an attempt to ensure that the increasing demand does not outgrow the proportion of production which can be made by the new process. Late development runs the risk of losing business to competitors who are quicker off the mark.

Personnel

Another major source of potential change is the manpower situation. In industrial countries it is usually realistic to assume that a supply of suitably educated or skilled manpower is available, but in developing countries this may not be so. In either case, changes in social attitudes may be important in affecting production conditions. For example, the reluctance of bank employees in the UK to work Saturdays, and the banks' difficulty in resolving this problem, has had major strategic implications. Partly for this, and partly for other reasons (such as the payment of interest), the building societies were able to capture business among just those manual workers who constituted the largest source of potential new bank customers.

Perhaps the most pervasive changes connected with the labour supply are connected with the position of women. Until recently, attitudes towards employment, particularly of skilled or professional staff, were based entirely on the lifelong career pattern of men. It was assumed without question that (except for the unforeseen interruption of unemployment) employees would work continuously throughout their working lifetimes, rising gradually to the plateau of responsibility on which they would spend the remainder of their careers. Quite clearly, for women the pattern is different: typically, a period of five to ten years' full-time work, an interval of no or part-time employment while having children below school age, and then a return to part- or full-time work.

Legislation and the hardening of attitudes against sex discrimination at work will increasingly compel more employers to see this pattern as something to be taken for granted and built into their personnel policy – a process being accelerated where there are shortages of labour. Moreover, just as men are now demanding the same retirement age as women, so at least a minority of men will seek the same flexibility of conditions of employment that women are being offered.

More fundamentally, such developments are gradually making people aware of the arbitrary nature of the concept of a standard working week, from which employees should diverge only in exceptional circumstances. This is most easily apparent in organisations which operate round the clock, like hospitals, petrol stations or hotels. The division of the work to be done into individual jobs does not necess arily involve everybody working the same number of hours per week. There is far more scope than has hitherto been recognised for matching the hours that the individual

woman (or man) wishes to work to the needs of the organisation. The idea of a hard and fast distinction between full
and part-time workers is rapidly becoming out-dated. Thus
one of the most significant changes in employment conditions will be the erosion of distinctions between full-time
and part-time employment and the need for management
to take a flexible attitude towards individuals' hours of
work.

It is sometimes suggested that the full-time workers will
constitute the privileged, hard core of management and the
part-time workers will represent an underprivileged prolet-
ariat.[4] This may have been a feature of part-time work,
particularly part-time casual jobs, in the past. But in so far
as the pressure now is to induce women with valuable skills
or expertise to continue work while their children are
young, the firm has an interest in treating them as part of
the permanent work-force. Moreover, organisations like
the banks must of necessity regard their part-time workers
as regular, not casual, workers. In addition equal opportunities legislation and economic and social pressures are
going to force employers to give part-time workers equal
treatment (pro-rata, of course) as regards pensions, holidays,
annual increments etc.

Such developments will tend to weaken the rather rigid
hierarchical systems which are still the norm in most large
firms – in particular the assumption that, once having
reached a certain level, you must always be employed at
that level or higher or be regarded as a failure, and conversely
the assumption that continuity of progress up the promotion
ladder is essential.

Fuel and Material Supplies

The potential impact of external developments on the availability and cost of materials is the third major area of
environmental assessment. As far as fuel and energy are
concerned, this is one of the most dynamic and least stable
areas for examination in the light of developments since
OPEC became effective. For many industries, the impact
of oil developments on the world economic situation may
be more important than the price of fuel in itself, but for

certain industries (e.g. air transport) changes in fuel prices *per se*, either absolute or relative, are important. In many cases supplies of materials are not a critical environmental factor, but even some quite ordinary materials may suffer marked changes in price or availability, for example minerals and by-products. There may be limited sources of supply (e.g. of chrome), so that political developments in the regions where that supply is located may need careful watching.

Finance

Changes in the financial situation, particularly the availability and cost of borrowing, are difficult to forecast for any prolonged period ahead: so too are exchange rates, which may be of vital importance to businesses engaged in export, or even the home-orientated business subject to foreign competition.

Changes in tax laws and government policy in giving financial assistance to industry may be of considerable strategic importance. With increasing freedom of capital movement, mobile investment in new plants is being increasingly sought after by governments and government institutions at all levels: the consequent financial incentives for new investment are becoming an important element in the location strategy of the large multinationals – as was seen, for example, by the Ford engine plant which was eventually located in South Wales.

Forecasting

One of the most widely read authors on management topics has declared that 'forecasting is not a respectable human activity and not worthwhile beyond the shortest of periods.'[5] This is an extreme view, but forecasting (particularly quantitative forecasting) has certainly come in for a great deal of criticism over the last decade – basically because so many economic forecasts turned out to be incorrect in the face of the oil crisis and the ensuing world recessions. Unfortunately, the need for forecasting will not go away merely because forecasting is difficult and fraught with error. (I refrain from saying forecasting has become *increasingly* difficult because it has always seemed difficult. There was a long-standing joke in the Treasury, going back to at least the 1950s, that the annual report on the balance of payments forecasts always began: 'This year is a particularly difficult one in which to forecast the balance of payments.')

The fundamental reason why forecasting is unavoidable is that many business decisions require years to take their full effect — particularly investment in various forms (e.g. new plant, the development of new processes and new products). It follows that such decisions have to be made in the light of possible future conditions, and some estimate must be made of the impact expected from them. In many cases forecasts of future conditions and the impact of the decisions in question are inescapably quantitative. This is most obviously true with decisions concerning the size of market and the volume of sales and capacity, but it also applies to the monetary as well as the physical aspects of such decisions, i.e. future prices, costs and profits. Hence, sooner or later the consideration of environmental changes has to be expressed in terms of their possible quantitative effects on such things as size of market, sales, selling prices, wages and material prices. We discuss the use of such forecasts for financial evaluation purposes in chapter 9.

Quantitative forecasting must be based on as thorough an analysis as possible of the past. This may at first sight seem an odd recipe for looking at the future, but it is not. One of the main features of inaccurate forecasts is that they are based solely on the present position (or, quite frequently a forecast of how the present year will turn out, because the figures are not available yet), so that the projections of the future are untrammelled by any data on the past. A well-known version of this is the so-called 'hockey-stick' forecast, in which the recent rate of expansion of say, sales is assumed to rise substantially in the forecast period, often with no adequate justification (figure 3.1). It is wise to be suspicious of forecasts of future growth which say nothing about the experience of recent years, and to be particularly careful about profit forecasts which start off with a projected figure

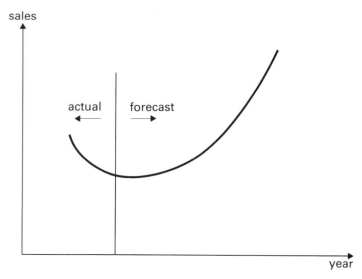

Figure 3.1 'Hockey stick' forecast

for the current or following year without any run of actual figures for the past.

In any examination of the past for forecasting purposes it is important, first, to determine how the variable to be forecast has in fact been moving in the past: has it been rising or falling, steadily or unsteadily, at what rate? Second, past data should be examined for possible causal links with other factors and their quantitative relationships — for example, how car sales were affected by changes in real personal disposable incomes.

Correlation analysis is a method of establishing whether there is evidence of any association between two variables and a statistical measure of the degree of such an association, such as the relation between the general price level and the quantity of money. *Regression analysis* is a method of establishing the magnitude of a change in one variable associated with a change in another; for example, if changes in the quantity of money and the general price level were associated, what change in the former is associated with a specified change in the latter? *Multiple regression analysis* provides a technique for establishing an equation relating the behaviour of the variable to be predicted to a number of determining variables with the closest fit to past data. For example, this may establish that whisky consumption can be explained largely by changes in (a) personal disposable incomes and (b) changes in the price of whisky, and estimate the probable percentage rise in consumption resulting from a 1 per cent increase in disposable incomes or a 1 per cent decrease in the price.[6]

Correlation and regression analyses are primarily techniques for use when there are no direct data linking one variable with another. Their weakness is that they cannot establish a causal relationship or indicate in which direction such a relationship might work (e.g., does the quantity of money reflect or cause a rise in prices?). In some cases the variable to be predicted (e.g. gas consumption) is in effect the sum of a number of sub-variables (e.g., gas consumption in the chemical and glass industries); then the problem is to determine the relationship between each sub-variable and the known determinants (e.g., output of different chemicals and processes employed).

There are two questions to be examined when using the analysis of the past to forecast the future. The first is whether a determining factor, say personal disposable income, can be expected to continue to behave in the future as it has done in the past. The second is whether the relationship between the determining factors and the variable being forecast is likely to change; for example, will car sales continue to bear the same relationship to personal disposable income?

A prime question in considering the future movement of key economic variables is whether there is likely to be any discontinuity − such as the 1970s oil crisis. It is very often at such a point that the more quantitative economic factors and the less quantitative political factors come together. Some macroeconomic discontinuities have no particular political causal factor: the 1929 New York stock market crash is a prime example. But very often economic discontinuities reflect political action, which frequently seems much less 'discontinuous' when viewed in long-run perspective than it does at the time, e.g. the spread of Muslim fundamentalism.

Macroeconomic forecasts in particular need to be explicitly related to the essential key political assumptions or forecasts. For example, many of the over-optimistic forecasts during the 1970s were based on the political assumption that governments would take expansionary action when unemployment rose substantially above previous levels. Unemployment at levels of 1 million, then 2 million and then 3 million were regarded as 'politically unacceptable'. The economic forecasts were based explicitly or implicitly on assumptions about government economic policy which did not foresee the dramatic change in the philosophy of economic management, and the adoption of drastically deflationary policies to combat price inflation together with an abandonment of the previous belief that demand management could and should be used to maintain full employment. In looking forward now, one of the possible discontinuities to consider is whether the relatively high level of unemployment will remain 'politically acceptable' as the long-term effect on the areas and communities involved take their toll.

Having taken a view on the key determining variables, which often include such key economic variables as gross domestic product, personal incomes or industrial production, the question remains whether the variable to be predicted will be related to them in the same way as in the past. For example, will consumption of plastics in the motor industry be related in the same way to the number of cars produced? Again, before considering the future, examine the past. How has consumption per car been behaving? What past and future trends are there in size of cars, engine and body design and the use of plastics versus other materials? In such a case it is possible to tackle the problem from at least two directions: overall figures for plastic consumption and car output, and detailed information about the materials used in different models. To arrive at a view about (average) consumption per car in future years, it is then necessary to

forecast the distribution of sales between different models
or size categories and to estimate other effects of model
changes.

With widely consumed and well-established products, like
gas or electricity, the relationship between consumption
and the key economic variables such as activity in the main
consuming industries does not vary greatly. Thus, the
economic variables become the key to forecasting demand,
and the accuracy of the demand forecasts reflects the
accuracy of the economic forecasts. But with relatively new
products, there may be no such stable relationships and
demand may be much more difficult to forecast.

In an uncertain world, any forecasts are subject to error.
Indeed, if there were no uncertainty, there would be no
forecasting: the future would be known like the past.
Uncertainty does not invalidate forecasts, but it does mean
that no forecast should be treated as a certainty. It is
essential to consider the variety of outcomes that may be
possible and to take a view as to their relative likelihood.
The great bugbear of forecasting is the 'single point' or
'one-line' forecast that is treated as a certainty − until it
fails to materialise. For presentational reasons there is always
pressure to limit the exploration of the future in this way,
but even where only one set of figures is presented it is
essential to treat them as only a typical or central point of a
range of possible outcomes.

Sensitivity Analysis

The simplest and best established method of recognising
the uncertain nature of forecasts is to consider a central
figure together with a higher and lower alternative which
are considered to be within reasonable bounds of probability. This is relatively straightforward where the decision
revolves around one key forecast, such as sales volume; but
it leads to complications where a number of key variables
are each subject to similar uncertainty, for example sales
volume, selling prices and labour costs. Permutating the
various possibilities soon proliferates the number of end
results, but very often, combining all the low figures and all
the high figures gives an improbably extreme end result (if

the different variables are unrelated). It is then necessary to adopt *sensitivity analysis* and examine the effect on the end result of variations in the key variables taken one at a time. This establishes the sensitivity of the end result to the possible variations in different factors and hence the need for further examination of the most critical factors or means of reaching a satisfactory outcome despite this uncertainty. Sensitivity and risk analysis is discussed further in connection with investment evaluation in chapter 9.

Scenarios

An alternative approach to the problem of uncertainty is *'scenario planning'* or the use of *'multiple scenarios'*. This consists, in essence, in painting a series of alternative pictures of the future and considering the impact on the enterprise and the response it should make. The concept has come to be interpreted in a variety of ways. Initially, a scenario was a 'hypothetical sequence of events' covering a number of years.[7] Latterly it has also been applied to snapshots of the future at a particular date. Most simply, a scenario is 'a description of a possible, or probable, future – in other words a forecast'.[8] In principle, a scenario should be internally consistent, the events of one year following from earlier developments, or the political and economic conditions in the snapshot year being mutually consistent.

The scope of the scenario will depend on the purposes for which it is conceived. For an international oil company it may be a wide-ranging picture of world political and economic developments. For a smaller company it may be much more limited. One of the purposes of the process is to stimulate thought about possible new developments which may affect the enterprise. Thus the process of formulating the scenario may be as important as the process of using it. Because the approach is, in a sense, deliberately fanciful, and because no particular probability is attached to the outcome, the construction of scenarios becomes a way of 'thinking the unthinkable'; that is, of looking at a view of the future to which no one is committed but which might just happen. In so far as it is easier to do this by means of scenarios rather than by examining a wider range of outcomes in the traditional forecasting process, the scenario approach can serve an important political process in large organisations. In such organisations the difficulty is generally not that no one has thought of some rather drastic change in events – they probably have; but the whole weight of authority and the decision-making process is directed towards weeding out the far-fetched and the improbable in order to narrow down the area of consideration to the point where the ultimate decision seems as inevitable as possible. The far-fetched alternative thus receives short shrift.

While the scenario technique is basically a qualitative one, focusing on the interplay of political, social and economic events, it can be used in a quantitative way. Having constructed different scenarios, say of economic and political developments, these can be expressed in terms of forecasts of gross domestic product, rates of inflation and unemployment, and then used to make alternative forecasts in the usual manner.

A leading protagonist of the scenario approach has been Shell, which started scenario planning in the early 1970s.[9] The planners in Shell have developed a hierarchy of global long-term and short-term scenarios looking at world-wide development and a series of local scenarios concentrating on factors likely to affect different parts of the business. They have tended to produce two sharply contrasting global scenarios – when they produced three, too much emphasis was placed on the middle one. Beginning in 1977, the scenarios have included a broad analysis of social trends. In November 1978 Shell published descriptions of two long-term scenarios.[10] Scenario A envisaged weaker world economic growth and no real effort to solve the energy problem. Scenario B predicated strong economic growth on a world-wide scale, and effective measures to save energy. The scenarios examined the possible state of the energy market in each of the three decades up to the year 2010. They also projected energy demand in the UK in 2010 on each of the two scenarios.

Whether by the use of alternative scenarios, sensitivity analysis or merely considering a range of figures, the key to coping with uncertainty is to explore the implications of more than one set of figures. Success in assessing the possible impact and opportunities of environmental change is not a matter of 100 per cent forecasting accuracy (that is only a matter of luck), but of judging correctly the broad factors at work and the approximate time-scale over which they will become effective. Quantitative forecasts provide an important discipline in this process as long as they do not lead to unjustified expectations as to their accuracy.

Notes

1 An excellent discussion of these issues (mainly in an American context), including the legal status of the employees of the corporation, first published 31 years ago but still as relevant today is Edward S. Mason (ed.), *The Corporation in Modern Society*, 1959.
2 Richard Tanner Pascale and Anthony Athos, *The Art of Japanese Management*, 1982, chapter 2.
3 Charles W. Hofer and Dan Schendel, *Strategy Formulation: Analytical Concepts*, 1978, p. 91.
4 See, for example, Charles Handy, *The Age of Unreason*, 1989, 'All organisations will soon be Shamrock organisations', p. 25.
5 Peter F. Drucker, *Management*, 1977, p. 118 of Pan paperback edition.
6 See, for example, J. J. Thomas, *An Introduction to Statistical Analysis for Economists* (2nd edn), 1983.
7 Herman Kahn and Anthony Wiener, *The Year 2000*, 1978.
8 Rochelle O'Connor, *Multiple Scenarios and Contingency Planning*, 1978.
9 Christopher Lorenz, 'How Shell Made Its Managers Think the Unthinkable' and 'Shell Strikes a Refined Way of Exploring the Future', *Financial Times*, 4 and 5 March 1980. Shell's scenarios in the first half of the 1970s are also discussed in 2 articles by Pierre Wack, 'Uncharted Waters Ahead' and 'Shooting the Rapids', *Harvard Business Review*, September/October and November/December 1985.
10 'Tomorrow's Energy' and '1990 and Beyond', summarised by René D. Zentner in 'Scenarios, Past, Present and Future', *Long Range Planning*, June 1982.

4

Assessing the Situation of the Company

In the simple model for formulating strategy set out at the end of chapter 1, the third step was to take stock of the situation of the company and assess its strengths and weaknesses. Such an 'audit' of the current position is an essential preliminary to consideration of how the company can most fruitfully respond to possible future changes in external factors and the threats and opportunities they pose. Drawing up a strategy is about tackling the future, but it must be based on a realistic appraisal of the company's past and present performance. Any strategy or plan which plunges straight into projections of the future without any proper appreciation of past trends or the current situation should be treated with a good deal of suspicion. Yet considerations of space, a desire to hold the readers' interest, the number of columns permissible in a statistical table and sheer laziness often conspire to produce an elaborate analysis of the future without any correspondingly detailed picture of the past.

Financial Performance

The first essential in taking stock of a company's past and current performance is to examine the profit, revenue and cost figures for recent years, together with the latest forecast for the current year. The need is not merely to observe the actual results but to analyse and understand the factors underlying them. This applies both to the profits of the company as a whole and to the profits attributable to particular activities or product groups: in the case of large companies these may be separately organised in divisions

or subsidiaries, but even so organisational boundaries do not generally provide a sufficiently detailed subdivision for this purpose.
  To take a typical manufacturing company as an example, the key questions on the revenue side concern changes in:

1 volume or quantity of sales (i.e. after allowing for price movements);
2 product and quality mix;
3 destination (i.e. markets or customers);
4 prices of specific products in particular markets.

It is necessary to examine these factors over a period of, say, five years, and identify so far as possible the key determinants of the changes.
  Similarly, on the cost side the key elements for such a firm would be:

1 volume of production;
2 product and quality mix;
3 manufacturing efficiency;
4 prices of inputs (e.g. labour, materials, fuel, etc.).

Standard Costs as a Yardstick

Where, as in most major companies, there is a *standard cost system*, this provides an invaluable tool for analysing cost changes. A standard cost system divides the operation into a number of cost centres, each of which will have a target or 'standard' cost per unit of output. This standard cost will be set for a specific volume of production with specified 'input prices' − prices of materials, services, etc., and labour costs per hour. An integral part of the standard costs will be technical standards − the consumption of such inputs per unit of output at a specified level of activity, as determined by rates of manning, fuel and material usage, scrapping, etc.
  The use of standard costs for analysing the movement of costs falls into two parts. The first is the analysis of changes in standard costs (which will generally be revised annually). Such changes will reflect (a) changes in 'input' prices, whether arising from inflation or from changes in 'real'

prices (changes in prices corrected for inflation, i.e. by an index of the general price level) and (b) changes in technical standards, that is, in the consumption of such inputs per unit of output at a specific level of activity.

The second element in the analysis is to examine the extent to which actual costs have varied from standard costs each year – generally called *variance analysis*. Such variances may result from deviations in activity from the standard level specified in the standard cost data; for example, an 'activity variance' may reflect either production difficulties or demand factors. A second major grouping may be termed 'manufacturing variances', which relate to differences in technical standards. A third constitutes 'buying-in variances' in the input prices of labour, materials, etc. The size and direction of all these variances need examination, in particular to see whether there is any systematic bias. If, for example, manufacturing variances are persistently adverse, operating standards are being consistently set too high; it is then important to bear this in mind and to try to eliminate such over-optimism in any future cost forecasts.

Profitability: Return on Capital

What has been said so far relates to the profits generated by the various activities of the company. These then have to be related to the capital invested. In particular, profitability needs to be measured against the replacement value of the fixed (and working) capital employed. As was explained in chapter 2, in times of inflation, rates of return on the historic cost of capital can be misleading, particularly if the plant has been written down more rapidly for accounting purposes than economic obsolescence would indicate. It is quite common to find activities showing an apparently satisfactory high rate of return on a low capital base that is quite unsatisfactory when measured against the replacement cost of capital. This is especially true when markets are relatively stagnant and no major expansion schemes are in progress in the industry in question.

Cash Flow and Financing

Next to profitability, the second aspect of a company's financial strength or weakness is its cash flow or liquidity position. In the very short term this is the most fundamental aspect because it determines whether or not the firm is bankrupt or can continue trading. In the longer run, however, it is subsidiary to profitability in the sense of the ability of the company to earn an adequate return on capital and hence attract and remunerate additional funds. One particular aspect of cash flow analysis in a conglomerate, or a firm where the financing of different businesses can be separated, is to distinguish those activities that are net generators of cash from those that are net absorbers of cash. (The implications of this are discussed in chapter 6 on Portfolio Analysis.)

A company generating a steady cash surplus will obviously be in a strong position to expand by acquisition or investment in new plant. A company requiring net injections of cash, even though showing a good profitability record, will have to consider means of raising further capital as a key aspect of any strategy. This raises in turn the ability of the company to remunerate new capital, which depends on its current profits in relation to interest and dividend payments. The existing capital structure (in particular, the debt/equity ratio) will also affect the possible form of any new financing. These are all, of course, by their nature characteristics of the company as a whole rather than of its component activities.

Financial Standing

The third aspect of a firm's financial standing is its stock market position and its general ability to raise additional finance. The stock market's assessment will be affected both by the firm's earnings record and by its dividend policy. A reasonably buoyant share price is, generally speaking, a source of strength, reducing the likelihood of take-over bids and opening up the possibility of raising additional capital by further share issues. The ability to raise money by further borrowing is another major point to be taken into account in making a strategic assessment: if a firm wishes to borrow funds, its existing debt/equity ratio must not be excessive and its general profitability must be satisfactory.

The financial strengths and weaknesses of the firm are critical. The profitability aspect sums up the financial effects of all the other factors, and the financial position influences both the type of strategy needed and the type of strategy it is possible to pursue. A poor financial position makes the need for financial improvement the dominating factor, in the extreme case in order to avoid bankruptcy. A strong financial position gives the widest field of manoeuvre in formulating strategy, and the most room to expand by acquisition or investment.

Products and Markets

Product Life Cycle

The nature and quality of a firm's products are two of its greatest sources of strength or weakness. They need to be considered in relation to developing markets and technology, both in their own right and in comparison with competitors' products. The idea of the *product life cycle* is a useful concept for this purpose. It consists simply of regarding products as going through a life cycle of birth, rapid growth, maturity, and decline or death. This process is most characteristic of durable products involving technological innovation; black and white television sets are a classic example. The rapid growth takes place while ownership per household of the new product is increasing; then sales tend to flatten out as ownership reaches saturation point and demand is mainly for replacement; decline follows when the product is outdated by further innovation − in this case, colour television. For products of this type, including the so-called 'mechatronic' products (volume-produced engineering products, ranging from computers to engineering), it is important to consider what stage the firms' products have reached in their life cycle.[1]

The cash flow and profits attributable to the product

follow a related but different curve to the volume of sales (see figure 4.1). The initial cash flow will be negative while money is being invested in developing the product and setting up the necessary production facilities. Even when production has started, the initial low volume of production and teething problems may at first involve a loss. But as large-scale production gets under way, profits will rise. There will, however, be some offsetting cash requirements for building up stocks and working capital, and as time goes by, for further investment to enlarge productive capacity.

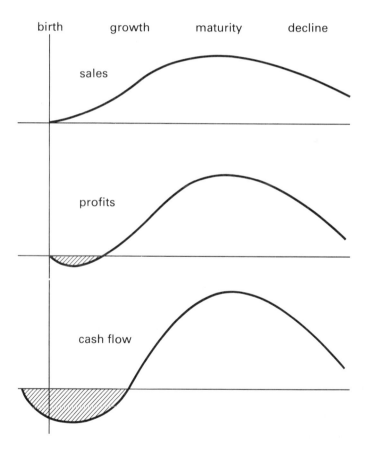

Figure 4.1   Product life cycle

As the product reaches maturity and sales begin to rise more slowly, or flatten out, profits will become more stable and capital requirements decrease. At this stage, cash flow may reach its peak. Profits are likely to decrease if the product passes from maturity to a period of decline, as it is supplanted by further innovation, but cash flow may remain high if investment is kept to the minimum. At some point, however, continued decline and intense competition between the remaining producers will lead to declining profits and eventually to losses.

While this concept is a pertinent one for certain products, it would be a mistake to assume that all products go through such a life cycle. Many do not. There may be an initial period of rapid growth, followed by a period of slower increase in sales, but not necessarily followed by any decline. Many staple products go on indefinitely with only periodic changes in the precise nature of the products, for example bread, steel and houses.

It is thus important to distinguish between life cycles in (a) individual brands, (b) models or varieties of products and (c) the class of product in general. Clearly the cycle is more likely to occur in the first two cases than the last.

Product Range

The extent of a firm's product range needs particularly careful analysis. A wide product range can help secure customers or outlets, and makes advertising less costly per unit. On the other hand, the inclusion of 'unprofitable' items for the sake of maintaining a comprehensive range is a potential weakness. What is or is not an 'unprofitable' product in a related range of products is not, however, easy to determine. The key issue is the extent to which sales of other products depend on that in question. Frequently, a retailer or industrial purchaser will want to buy his whole range of requirements from one source, and an incomplete product range will make him more likely to shift part or all of his requirements in that range to a competing supplier.

There is thus an important distinction between unprofitable activities or product groups and ostensibly unprofitable items within a product group. It is, of course, essential to try to limit the number of items within a product range to the minimum that will serve the customers' requirements, rather than (as so often happens) let the number multiply as fresh items are brought into the catalogue without considering others for deletion. But in general, a complete product range is a source of strength in getting an adequate share of the market.

Related to the question of product range is the practice of 'bundling', i.e. only selling a group of complementary products as one bundle and not making them available separately.[2] For example, colour films were originally only sold inclusive of processing. They have now been 'unbundled' and the film is sold as one product and developing and printing as another.

A bundling strategy can be a source of strength if there are economies involved, or if in the case of servicing, bundling guarantees the satisfactory operation of the product. It may, however, make the producer vulnerable if he insists on supplying a service that a specialist can provide more cheaply or satisfactorily. There is a tendency, particularly with technical products, for the extent of bundling to diminish as the products become more widely known and competition develops from specialist producers of components or servicing engineers. Consumers' perception as to what constitutes a 'product' may also change over time.

Marketing

By 'marketing strength', we mean strength relative to competitors. This can spring from a variety of factors: competitive prices and high quality are the most obvious. Where the product is not easily distinguishable from its competitors price is very important, but it is difficult for the firm to charge a perceptibly different price from its competitors. The greater the differentiation in product, either real or apparent, the more scope there is for manoeuvre in setting prices relative to competitors. Pricing strength may be used either to secure a high market share by keen pricing or to secure high margins by exploiting any potential for differential pricing to the full.

Market share − the ratio of the company's sales of the

product in question to total sales in that particular market — has for some years been regarded as the major indicator of strength or weakness, and a great deal of oversimplified analysis and prescription has been built upon this assumption (see discussion of porfolio analysis in chapter 6). The achievement of a high market share will generally reflect a firm's competitive success in preceding years — although it may also be the result of merging a number of companies. In addition, with a relatively new product it may reflect the fact that the firm was first in the field. But whatever factors may have established such a position, a high market share is not necessarily a straightforward source of future competitive strength (as is often suggested). It may involve a strong competitive position where the firm in question is the 'price-leader' (i.e. initiates changes in prices) and also is able to dictate the frequency and nature of the introduction of new models or products; it may also be associated with economies of scale from a large operation.

On the other hand, high market share can be a source of vulnerability. The firm with a very high market share is something of a sitting duck, waiting to be shot at by smaller firms willing to give special price concessions or service. The large competitor has great powers of retaliation, but it may be difficult to use them to defeat a small competitor without a public row or infringing laws about price discrimination. A very high market share may also attract anti-monopoly investigations by government regulatory agencies: and it can mean a greater risk of the market share going down with little or no scope for raising it.

A small firm with a low market share often has the ability to out-manoeuvre its larger competitors; it can adopt more flexible pricing policies and in many circumstances has a wider range of possible ways of expanding its share. On the other hand, where advertising and building up a brand-image are important, the low-volume competitor is at a disadvantage. He may also be vulnerable to being shut out of parts of the market (e.g. selling to supermarket chains) by aggressive selling by a large competitor.

In analysing potential strengths and weaknesses, competitive strength, particularly future competitive strength, should not be regarded as being simply proportional to market share. The direction in which it is moving (i.e. whether it is growing or shrinking) may be more important. It is essential to analyse the reasons for, and implications of, the market share in question.

Other marketing factors that should be assessed include:

- **Distribution network** (e.g. transport and warehouse facilities): an established network may have potential for distributing a wider range of products.
- **Servicing facilities**: these may be very important for certain types of product, particularly where industrial customers need a specialist service. Servicing of individual customers tends to be in the hands of retailers, local repairers, etc., but a repair service run by the manufacturers themselves can be an attraction.
- **General reputation**: a well-known company name or brand-image may make it much easier to introduce new products.
- **Market research ability**: a good record in matching new products to market requirements is an essential strength in fields where products and models are continually changing.
- **Patent protection**: expiring patents may pose a threat to existing products.
- **Pricing structure and policy**: the firm's ability to secure adequate prices will depend partly on the pricing structure of the industry and partly on the position of the firm within the industry. Capital-intensive industries, like steel, frequently have weak pricing structures because of the pressure to cut prices in order to increase volume when plant is underutilised. This tendency is stronger, the more uniform the product – or where indirect forms of product differentiation, such as delivery or quality, represent an extra cost. Industries with more variety between the products of different firms provide greater choice of pricing policy.

Production

Costs

Production costs will depend on (a) the type of plant available and (b) the efficiency with which it is used. The age of plant is an important factor to consider. A new plant should be a source of strength, once the initial teething troubles have been overcome, provided it embodies the right production route and technology. But a nearly new plant based on a now outdated technology can be a serious embarrassment, as it makes it particularly difficult to get into the new technology. Misjudgements of this kind in capital-intensive industries can be nearly fatal.

Old plant, which is virtually obsolescent, is an immediate weakness, but the fact that it has to be replaced provides room for strategic manoeuvre; and unless the company has been running in blinkers, it will have been prepared for the need for capital expenditure in the not-too-distant future. Middle-aged plant which has become outdated often presents the most difficult decisions.

Capacity

The firm's capacity in relation to the demand for its products is one of the most important factors in determining the nature of the strategic problem it faces. Shortage of capacity involves delays in meeting orders, lost sales and unless the product is very highly sought after (e.g. Rolls Royce cars), may soon involve an actual decline in sales. On the other hand, excess capacity or low utilisation drives up unit costs.

Ideally, the firm wants to be in a position where capacity is well-matched to sales, but with just enough flexibility to meet seasonal and other fluctuations. Changes in macroeconomic conditions, however, frequently lead to general conditions of capacity shortage or excess.

Where the excess of capacity can be remedied by closure of one of a number of plants, preferably the oldest or highest-cost, then closure may improve costs. But where, as in many medium-sized firms, there is only one plant producing any particular product, rationalisation of this kind is only possible in conjunction with other firms.

Supplies

Access to low-cost supplies, particularly of buying-in components or semi-finished products, can be an important source of strength, particularly in an international context. For an oil company, access to oil reserves is obviously a key consideration. Raw material supplies are particularly important for process industries.

Delivery and Quality

In many fields prompt delivery, reliable quality and efficient after-sales services are just as, or more, important than price in capturing and holding customers. The firm's performance in these respects needs to be rigorously assessed in establishing its current strengths and weaknesses.

Location

Location can be a key strategic factor. Existing location may limit the firm's strategic options: for example, an inadequate site may rule out any major extension of existing capacity. The choice of new locations either to expand capacity or enter new markets may be an important element in any new strategy.

Personnel

Has the firm got good industrial relations? Does production proceed without interruption? Are manning standards low? What is the prevalent attitude to changes in working methods? These are some of the key questions in the personnel field. In some well-known British firms, adverse answers to these questions represent the key strategic weaknesses of the enterprise. Conversely, for most Japanese firms this is a major source of strength.

The management skills and resources in the firm are crucial to its future. Weaknesses are often most apparent in small firms, which have outgrown the capacity of the original founder to manage without the support of professional management in greater depth. But in quite large companies there may also be a shortage of the appropriate managers or inadequate provision for succession.

Technical Factors

The assessment of a firm's technical strengths and weaknesses should cover its existing products and methods of production, together with its research and development (R and D) capability both for new products and for improved methods of production. Weaknesses in existing products or production techniques may be remedied either from within or from outside the firm according to the R and D resources at its command. This distinction between a capacity for developing products and a capacity for developing production methods may be a crucial one strategically. A distinctive feature of the successful Japanese attack on world markets for many products has been their continued development both of new products and of methods of mass-producing them cheaply, thus giving them a dual advantage. This contrasts, for example, with the Sinclair strategy for computer development, of concentrating on product development and relying on competitive subcontracting to get it produced.

Company Audit

Corporate Character

To complete the company audit, there remains a final question. What are the general corporate strengths and weaknesses of the enterprise? For a few firms, these are clear. For example, Marks and Spencer have a distinctive managerial expertise in buying and merchandising which they successfully extended from clothing to a wider range of goods. But most firms do not have such clear-cut managerial specialty, and any assessment conducted internally should avoid the danger of wishful thinking that the firm is especially strong at whatever top management fancies it wants to do.

The general image and reputation of a company are important, particularly in politically sensitive fields such as pharmaceuticals. A key question is whether the enterprise has a record of success in reaching the objectives it has set itself. Has it the ability to adapt to changing circumstances?

Last but not least, has the firm the right organisation for its size, type of business and general circumstances?

Company Profile

The idea of taking stock of a company's position by identifying its 'strengths and weaknesses' has become firmly established in the literature as one of the basic steps in formulating long-term strategy. It is more a tool for the occasional fundamental review, particularly when outside consultants are called in, than for the regular annual or periodic updating of a firm's long-term strategy and plans. The process of an audit or stocktaking as an aid to setting future objectives is, or should be, however, more refined than the rather black and white, good and bad concepts of strengths and weaknesses. The less emotive concept of assessing the *profile* or characteristics of the firm might in some cases be more productive. Very often, an accurate perception of why the firm is successful at present may reveal a number of characteristics which are difficult to categorise in such black and white terms.

For example, a small service engineering firm has excellent relations with its principal customers. This rests on the fact that one of the joint owners and managing directors has built up the firm from scratch, is well-known in local business circles and knows his customers personally. They telephone him direct and he has no one in the office that is generally recognised as being capable of standing in for him.

The firm is doing very well and thinking of extending its activities. Its present good relations with its customers cannot be categorised simply as a 'strength' to be built on. Dealing with more customers from a wider area would be beyond the scope of the present intensely personal nature of the organisation. The 'strength' of the present good and highly personalised customer relations is fully exploited, and could turn into a weakness if taxed beyond its limits. Thus it does not inevitably follow that a strong feature of the present situation is necessarily a pillar that can support further extension. Current strengths may be something that need preservation or consolidation.

Again, having identified a firm's weaknesses, these may become either priorities for change, or something to live with and minimise. Poor location, for example, may be a weakness, but to move a firm lock, stock and barrel may not be feasible. If the age of machinery is a weakness, it may be fairly easy to replace. On the other hand, if traditional working practices are the problem, they may be much more difficult to eradicate. Elimination of weaknesses is desirable, but making a new strategy heavily dependent on reversing some longstanding weakness may be precarious.

Notes

1 See Merlin Stone, 'Competing with Japan – The Rules of the Game', *Long Range Planning*, April 1984.
2 See Michael E. Porter, *Competitive Advantage*, 1985, chapter 12.

5

Diversification

The main aim of making an assessment of the capabilities of the firm is to use it as a basis for determining the directions which any new strategy should take. Having made as objective and realistic an assessment as possible, the next step is to consider the implications of this assessment for future strategy, taking into account the parallel assessment of possible environmental change.

One of the most common strategies is investment in new facilities, or acquisition of another company, in order to produce additional products; this is commonly known as *diversification*. Diversification consists of broadening the company's product mix to include products differing significantly from its original or basic product lines — for example, a typewriter company branching out to sell computers. The basic motivations for diversification are (a) to move into products offering a higher level of return and (b) to spread the risks of products either running into temporary difficulties or reaching the end of their life cycle.

Synergy

In considering possible new initiatives involving diversification, a useful analytical tool for considering critically the relation between the capabilities required from the new initiative and the existing capabilities of the company is the concept of *synergy*.

Synergy is said to exist where it is more advantageous to combine two or more activities than to undertake them separately; it is frequently described as '2 + 2 = 5'. For example, it may be cheaper and more effective to produce two products in one factory than to make them individually.

Types of Synergy

Synergy in business activity can occur in a variety of ways.

Sales and distribution   In sales and distribution, synergy is most likely to be significant where the products are both related and sold through the same outlets − for example, Dunlop tennis balls and racquets. In such cases, there are savings on advertising, sales administration and distribution. On the other hand, where the products are related but sold through different outlets, the synergy may be negligible; you would not, for example, expect to sell soap powder for washing machines in shops (or departments) selling the machines themselves − the powder is bought regularly but machines are bought only at infrequent intervals. Synergy may be exploited in a more limited way by the use of a common and well-advertised brand name; for example, the use of 'Dunhill', a brand name originally famous for pipes, for a diversity of products. It may also arise from the use of a common distribution or transport system, as when the Distillers' Company Limited linked the sale of baker's sundries to the distribution of yeast.

Production and investment   The most clear-cut form of synergy (and the least difficult to quantify in money terms) is economies of scale in production. In the steel industry, for example, the optimum scale of production for liquid steel is greater than that for rolling many steel products; it therefore reduces production costs to have multi-product plants with one steel-making plant and more than one finishing mill. There are, however, diseconomies of scale, particularly in human terms, as plants and organisations grow bigger; so it is important to consider whether the economies of scale being discussed are significant in relation to the less tangible disadvantages of large-scale operations.

Finding uses for by-products is another important form of synergy − using slag from steel plants for road-making, for example, or bran from flour for health foods.

Research and development   Synergy in research and development may exist where work in developing one process, product or material can serve as a basis for other new developments.

Purchasing   Savings in purchasing seem likely only where purchasing is a major element in the total activity of the firm, such as merchanting or importing.

Management   Synergy in management tends to be strongest for similar products, such as the entry of the clearing banks into the mortgage business. It may also arise where management resources are underemployed. A good example was the diversification of Davy Loewy (a leading British steel plant producer) into process plant design, thus making fuller use of their general management and technical resources and minimising the potentially disastrous effect of cyclical fluctuations in investment in the steel industry.

One of the traps in seeking management synergy is that the additional activities proposed may be genuinely related, but may take up too much time and effort and detract from the efficient execution of existing responsibilities. Overseas consulting is a case in point, particularly in the more pleasant parts of the world to visit! The amount of top management time devoted to overseas consulting subsidiaries may be quite disproportionate to their turnover or profitability – partly because of the endless demands for meetings with members of governments and officials from countries with which business may never materialise.

Corporate relations   A further form of synergy is that arising from a firm's external relations. For example, if a multinational company already has close relations with a particular government, it may seek to extend its overseas investment in that country into new fields. This rather tenuous link should be treated with caution and distinguished from extending sales to a particular government or government agency from one product to another.

Concentrating on one purchaser, such as the government or local authorities, again leads to a vulnerability to any reduction in purchasing by that body, for example government expenditure cuts.

Synergy through linked technologies creates a similar vulnerability, to the danger of their both being superseded simultaneously. This applies both to products and to methods of production.

The use of Synergy

In considering the possible benefits of synergy it is essential to analyse carefully, and as far as possible quantitively, the efforts of undertaking related activities. In what is still the best introduction to synergy, Ansoff's *Corporate Strategy*, he emphasises the need to approach synergy in rigorous analytical terms, estimating the benefits in additional revenue, or savings in costs or investments, wherever possible.[1]

This rigorous approach contrasts with the looser and more dangerous approach of asking, 'What business are we in?' The question encourages facile answers which can either be successful or disastrous − the latter frequently because they create the illusion of synergy where none exists. A typically dangerous answer is 'the leisure business': this encompasses such a variety of activities, many of them totally unrelated, as to be merely meaningless. It is one thing for a firm such as Rank, which has successfully diversified into a number of such activities, to say after the event that it is in 'the leisure business', but such a statement provides little useful guidance to a firm starting out on the path of diversification.

Even Drucker, who maintains strongly that 'strategy requires knowing "what our business is and what it should be"', also warns that it is 'almost always a difficult question and the right answer is usually anything but obvious'; indeed, 'there is never one right answer'.[2]

More recently Porter attributed the declining enthusiasm for the idea of synergy to 'the inability of companies to understand and implement it, not because of some basic flaw in the concept. . . Compelling forces are at work, however, that mean that firms must re-examine their attitude toward synergy. Economic, technological and competitive developments are increasing the advantage to be gained by those firms that can identify and exploit interrelationships among distinct but related businesses'.[3]

Synergy versus Risk

Synergy and risk are closely interrelated, in that certain types of synergy increase the vulnerability of the firm to risk. This applies particularly to market and technological synergy (which may overlap). *Market synergy*, arising from selling goods and services to the same customers to meet similar needs, involves the risk that both products may be hit simultaneously by a fall in demand arising from changes in economic circumstances, fashion or habit. For example, sales of both tennis racquets and balls will suffer if tennis goes out of fashion or the number of courts available declines. A firm selling squash racquets and balls as well will be rather safer, but could be hurt by similar trends.

Types of Diversification

There are two types of diversification. The first is into *related* products, where the firm is seeking to exploit synergy in marketing, production, technology or other fields. ICI is a classic case here; starting with heavy inorganic chemicals (alkalis, explosives and dyestuffs), it gradually diversified into heavy organics, paints, pharmaceuticals and synthetic fibres. Such diversification can come about either by investment by the original company or by acquisition of other companies in related fields. The second type of diversification is into *unrelated* products, in this case generally by acquiring other companies already engaged in these fields. This type of diversification was originally associated with the conglomerate movement in the United States which got under way in the 1960s. Between 1959 and 1969 the proportion of the 500 largest US companies diversified into unrelated products grew from 6.5 per cent to 19.4 per cent,[4] and by 1980 it had reached over 33 per cent.[5] The process was slower in the UK, but by 1980 the proportion of the 200 largest industrial companies in this category had reached around 18 per cent.[6]

Firms may be classified according to the degree and nature of their diversification. By 'degree' we mean the proportion of their total activity accounted for by diversified products. Rumelt adopts the following criteria.[7]

1 *Single business*: firms deriving over 95 per cent of their revenue from one product line.
2 *Dominant business*: firms deriving over 70 per cent of their revenue from one product line.
3 *Related businesses*: firms deriving less than 70 per cent of their revenue from their largest product line but whose product lines are related in some way, for example in terms of market, production or technology.
4 *Unrelated businesses*: firms deriving less than 70 per cent of their revenue from their largest product line and whose product lines are unrelated.

Rumelt further subdivided these second and third categories to distinguish 'related' diversification into: (a) 'constrained' or 'controlled' diversification into products all closely related both to the main product line and to each other; and (b) 'linked' diversification, in which each product is linked to another but they are not all interrelated. In an analysis of financial performance of the 500 largest US companies in the 1960s, he found that companies following a policy of controlled diversification showed the highest average return on capital, with the less diversified 'dominant' product companies doing rather better on average than the 'related' product companies. The former sub-group had a return on capital of 12.7 per cent and the latter of 12.0 per cent, against an average of 10.5 per cent.[8]

The unrelated product companies or conglomerates showed a lower return on capital than average (9.5 per cent). But when divided into conglomerates with active acquisition policies, securing an average annual growth of sales of over 20 per cent, and 'passive' companies, with an average growth rate of only 6 per cent, there was a significant difference in the rate of return on equity capital: 13.1 per cent for the former against 10.4 per cent for the latter. They both, however, had a return on capital nearly 1 per cent below the average (9.4 per cent for the passive and 9.6

per cent for the active conglomerates). These two comparisons suggest the obvious conclusion that the active conglomerates were more successful in terms of financial manipulation than industrial efficiency.

In a later study covering the period 1955−74, Rumelt developed his previous analysis to allow for the effects of differing average profitability in the industries in which the sample firms were involved. This confirmed the earlier results with rates of return lower by 3 to 4 percentage points for unrelated than related diversification.[9]

Assessing the success of diversification in spreading risk, in the sense of variability of earnings, Rumelt found that 'carefully controlled diversity is the best form of diversification for reducing fluctuations in earnings.' He suggested this was because such diversification involved a conscious attempt to replace products at the end of their life-cycle with new ones to meet the same continuing need. Widespread diversification left the firm still subject to the effects of macroeconomic fluctuations. The best hedge could be to concentrate on a few products whose fortunes were dependent on sections of the economy likely to move in different directions, such as government expenditure on defence and civilian consumption.

Data for later periods show less clear-cut advantages for related diversification and it may be that management were beginning to learn from earlier mistakes. A follow-up study of 71 US firms in Rumelt's sample covering the later period 1977−81 showed no clear advantage for related diversification, partly because unrelated diversified firms' profits held up better in the post 1979 recession.[10] Nor did there appear to be any significant differences in risk (as evidenced by fluctuations in profits) between these categories. An investigation into 305 large British companies over the period 1972−84 showed diversified businesses as being more profitable than single or dominant businesses but no clear distinction between the success of related or unrelated diversification.[11]

The results reflect not merely any success or the lack of it in managing the enlarged business, they also reflect the *prices* paid for any acquisitions. One key to success in any form of diversification is to have the skill and knowledge to avoid paying too high a price for new business. The second major moral may be partly that the fashion for indiscriminate diversification waned in the 1970s and 1980s, but also that well-conceived and successful diversification may follow a variety of avenues.

Related Diversification

Much of the analysis required to make decisions on diversification into related fields has already been discussed in chapters 3 and 4. First, it is necessary to consider the impact of future environmental change on the company's existing products and hence its financial prospects if it continues with its present products. If it is then considered that diversification may be desirable, possible new products need to be investigated in the light of the market and other changes projected, and the resources available for diversification. This is the point at which a realistic picture of the company's capabilities, function by function, is most essential.

Successful diversification into related products requires management resources appropriate for coping with the new product and synergy in one or more key fields (such as marketing, production or research and development). These two requirements are related but not identical. As discussed above, genuine synergy depends on common factors of some kind leading to cost savings or sales advantages if the new product is introduced. This does imply that managers who are used to selling or producing the existing line of products have relevant experience for handling the new products; but it does not necessarily follow that they can handle the new products without detriment to the existing business. It is also essential that top management have the resources to expand into new fields.

Such expansion can take two routes. The first is internal expansion, involving investment in the necessary facilities, and recruiting additional management and manpower to handle the new products within the company. The second is acquisition of another company already producing the products in question. To take the latter route requires not just the resources to assess and undertake such an acquisition, but also the ability to integrate it into the existing company to the extent needed to exploit any potential synergy.

For the diversification decision to have a reasonable chance of success, the preliminary stage of analysis and planning must not only define suitable products but also ensure that there are adequate resources (whether financial or managerial) to implement any such decision.

The considerations involved in establishing that potential new products are significantly related to existing ones are the same as those discussed when considering the potential existence of genuine synergy.

The market Do the products sell to the same customers? Are they sold or distributed through the same channels? Is there an existing brand name that will help to sell the new product? Will a wider range of products attract customers that at present buy all their requirements elsewhere?

Production Can the new products be produced on the same or related facilities? Will they fill up unused capacity? Will it be cheaper to produce the expanded range of products in one firm rather than separately?

Technology Can the existing resources devoted to research and development support the new products without commensurate increase in cost? (One of the reasons why related diversification tends to be more profitable is that it may increase the return on research and development expenditure.[12]) Do the new products reflect a more modern technology and hence represent potential replacements of the old?

General management Does the proposed diversification require the type of management appropriate to the existing business?

Finally, there is the question of whether the financial characteristics of the diversified activities promise a good 'fit' with those of existing products. If the company is already short of cash, diversifying into products requiring heavy investment will only make sense in special circumstances. If, on the other hand, the company has surplus cash, diversification into such areas may make good sense. Similarly, if the diversification is to be achieved by means of acquisition, the debt/equity ratio and other financial characteristics of the firm to be acquired need to be such as to improve rather than weaken the position of the firm making the acquisition.

Unrelated Diversification

Unrelated diversification tends to take the form of acquisition rather than direct investment, for the simple reason that the management of the diversifying firm has no experience in the area in question. Two kinds of investigation need to be undertaken to support such decisions. The first is to consider the general characteristics which any diversified activities should have if they are to strengthen the acquiring company, and hence the type of products that would be appropriate. The second is to examine the individual characteristics of any particular firm which is a candidate for acquisition. The first process may establish insurance as a preferred area, the second whether a particular insurance company is a good candidate for acquisition. Finally, of course, even if a candidate satisfies these two tests, it is only worth buying at the right price − a point which often seems in danger of going out of the window once battle is joined in a contested take-over! (The fact that acquisition decisions frequently appear to be made with very little supporting analysis, particularly in cases of contested take-overs, may be an important reason why unrelated diversification is somewhat suspect as far as financial results are concerned.)

In the analysis of initial fit, two underlying aspects of the portfolio analysis approach (see chapter 6) can be particularly helpful. The first is to focus on the implications for cash generation or requirement of the acquisition candidate in relation to the rest of the firm. The second is to raise the question as to how the life cycle of the proposed new product fits with those of existing products (see p. 62 above). In so far as new products require net investment and mature products generate cash, marrying the two can improve both the cash balance and diversify the spread of products over the life cycle. The portfolio approach is at its strongest in stimulating the search for a spread of products at different stages of development and with differing cash requirements.

Diversification of a firm making mature products into another (unrelated) mature product may be storing up trouble for the future, even if one product is a cash generator and the other requires investment. Unrelated diversification by a firm making new products into other new products of a similar vintage is also suspect.

How far the market growth/business strength matrix-type analysis used in the portfolio approach (discussed in chapter 6) acts as a reliable screen depends entirely on the validity of the market growth or profitability and business strength characterisations. Later developments of the so-called directional policy matrix approach have established points scoring systems for embodying various market characteristics and business characteristics into a total score for each business unit (see pp. 96–9). But it really seems more straightforward to drop the attractive simplicity of the two-way matrix, and catalogue directly the various relevant characteristics of (a) the market (such as rate of growth, average profitability, vulnerability to imports, etc.) and (b) the firm (such as its financial record, market share and apparent strengths and weaknesses). An acquisition profile can then be developed of the characteristics sought in a take-over candidate, including both the characteristics of the markets or industry in which it is operating and also the desirable features of the firm itself.

Perhaps even more than with related diversification, the profitability of unrelated acquisitions depends above all on the price paid – a point so obvious that it seems to attract remarkably little attention. One of the difficulties of running a successful policy of unrelated diversification is to find 'good bargains' in the market for companies.[13]

Benefits of Acquisition

It has to be recognised that the potential benefits of an acquisition vary according to whose interests are at stake. From the point of view of the development of the economy as a whole, there is only an advantage in a take-over or merger if some real economic benefit is obtained. The main way in which this may occur is if existing products are produced more economically or new products developed more rapidly, although other national economic aims might also be satisfied; for example, the country's international trade position strengthened.

In the 1980s acquisitions and mergers became increasingly dominated by short-term financial considerations and stock-market speculation. Industrial progress does not, however, result from people buying and selling existing businesses, but from developing and running them efficiently. The great American trust movement at the turn of the century involved large-scale buying and selling of businesses, but also the creation of enormous assets and operations for producing, distributing and selling oil. Those in developing countries, in particular, will appreciate that the reshuffling of existing businesses, whether flourishing or ailing, does not lie at the heart of the economic process. Whether acquisition or mergers produce any fundamental benefit to the economy at large depends on whether running the two separate businesses together produces higher incomes or lower costs than their operation as separate units.

Salter and Weinhold, in their wide-ranging study *Diversification through Acquisition*, argue that in the long run the shareholders also only benefit if additional real value is created — but in view of the short-term horizon of the stock market the immediate effects on share prices receive all the attention.[14] In a stimulating discussion of managers' and investors' objectives, however, they acknowledge that the two may diverge, although they conclude that managers' interests should be subordinated to investors' interests if the creation of economic value is to prevail in the long run.[15] The fact remains, however, that acquisitions that do not exploit any real economies or opportunities may still provide very real benefits to the acquiring management, if not to the management 'acquired'. The most basic is that control over a greater total of economic resources by heading a larger firm is likely to lead to very direct benefits to the managers concerned, both in terms of their emoluments and their industrial and social standing. Conversely, the top management in the company acquired may see themselves on the losing side in terms of their independence of action, although the most ambitious managers in the next layer down may benefit from the additional opportunities in a larger company. For ambitious managers, take-overs are a quicker route to expansion, with all the potential managerial benefits involved, than internal investment.

From the point of view of the employees, the benefits of acquisition depend not so much on whether there is any economic advantage, but on whether any such advantage takes the form of economies of scale and manpower-saving, as opposed to more rapid expansion through faster and more successful development. Moreover, there may well be a conflict of interest between employees in the two companies concerned if rationalisation of production involves increased production at one firm at the expense of manpower cuts at the other.

It must thus be recognised that acquisition decisions have an additional dimension to those involved in diversification by expanding the company's own activities, a fact reflected in the public attention they tend to receive. Such decisions involve the immediate and direct acquisition of economic power and resources, whether by negotiation or market contest, as opposed to the relatively gradual acquisition involved in expansion by investment. Thus, in organisational and human terms their consequences are different and more dramatic.

It is therefore important for managers considering acquisitions and mergers as a strategic weapon to make at least as thorough an analysis of the implications as in the case of a major investment project, and also to pay adequate attention to the organisational and human relations problems involved.

Notes

1 H. Igor Ansoff, *Corporate Strategy*, 1965, chapter 5.
2 Peter F. Drucker, *Management*, 1977, chapter 5.
3 Michael E. Porter, *Competitive Advantage*, 1985, chapters 9 and 10. Porter analyses synergy in the form of potential cost savings from 'sharing' production, distribution or supply activities, and goes on to develop the concept of 'horizontal strategy' to cover a firm's interrelated activities.
4 Richard P. Rumelt, *Strategy, Structure and Economic Performance*, 1974, table 2.2.
5 Derek F. Channon, 'Strategic Evolution and Portfolio Management Techniques', paper delivered to the Strategic and Long Range Planning Society, 1983.
6 Ibid.
7 Rumelt, *Strategy, Structure and Economic Performance*. Channon adopts a similar categorisation in his related study for the UK: Derek F. Channon, *The Strategy and Structure of British Enterprise*, 1973.
8 Rumelt, *Strategy, Structure and Economic Performance*, table 3.2.
9 Richard P. Rumelt, 'Diversification Strategy and Profitability', *Strategic Management Journal*, October–December 1982.
10 Yegmin Chang and Howard Thomas, 'The Impact of Diversification Strategy on Risk – Return Performance', *Strategic Management Journal*, May–June 1989.
11 Robert M. Grant and Azar P. Jammine, 'Performance Differences between the Wrigley/Rumelt Strategic Categories', *Strategic Management Journal*, July–August 1989.
12 Richard A. Bettis, 'Performance Differences in Related and Unrelated Diversified Firms', *Strategic Management Journal*, October–December 1981.
13 See Michael E. Porter, *Competitive Strategy*, 1980, pp. 350–7.
14 Malcolm S. Salter and Wolf A. Weinhold, *Diversification through Acquisition*, 1979.
15 Ibid., appendix to chapter 6.

6

Portfolio Analysis

'Portfolio analysis' approaches the problem of strategy formulation by treating the firm as an investor owning a collection of different businesses. These may be either organisational units, such as the subsidiaries of a holding company, or conceptual units for this purpose ('strategic business units'). Portfolio analysis is primarily concerned with the 'balance' or pattern of the firm's investments in different products or industries. The strategic problem for central management is regarded as that of determining which products or activities to expand or introduce and which to run down or sell off − in the extreme case, which businesses to acquire or dispose of − in order to get a balanced portfolio. The approach is thus primarily suitable for formulating strategy at the corporate level for large conglomerates or highly diversified firms, although it can also be applied to multi-product firms operating in a more limited field.

The limitation of portfolio analysis is that it is primarily concerned with which individual businesses should comprise the corporation, rather than how they are run, or even their individual long-term strategies (save in the very restricted sense as to whether they are to expand, be run down or even liquidated).

The Concept of Balance

The concept of a 'balanced' portfolio is concerned with three fundamental aspects of the business. The first is the net cash flow. The various businesses in the portfolio will have different cash-flow characteristics: some new and growing businesses, though profitable, will have a net demand for cash because of their investment requirements; other, more mature, businesses may be net generators of cash. Thus portfolio analysis is concerned with getting a balance of businesses with different cash-flow requirements which, when taken together, give an overall cash-flow position in harmony with the financial strategy of the company as a whole.

The second, and closely related, feature with which portfolio analysis is concerned is the stage of development which each business or product has reached.[1] The concept of 'balance' is based on the idea that differing cash-flow characteristics will be associated with different stages in the life cycle of different products (see pp. 62–4). A balanced portfolio will thus not only comprise businesses with complementary cash-flow characteristics, but also a collection of businesses in different stages of development, so that while some businesses based on older products are declining or dying, other growing businesses are beginning to take their place. Thus a balanced portfolio is designed to achieve corporate 'immortality' with the corporation itself surviving the decline and fall of the individual business units of which it is comprised.

The third aspect of balance is concerned with risk. One object in having a diverse portfolio of businesses is to reduce risk, in particular the risk of serious financial setback. To this end it is necessary to have a spread of activities in which the key market forces mainly affecting sales, but also in some cases supplies, differ. In particular, if sales of a particular business are cyclical, the ideal aim is to find another activity whose cycle is likely to be out of phase with the first. The major difficulty is that macroeconomic developments tend to affect the whole range of business activities, and even diversification between investment and consumer goods gives only limited protection from the risk of adverse economic developments.

One of the most widely used means of spreading risks is to diversify internationally, in the hope that different countries will be subject to different economic forces at any one time. There is considerable validity in this, in that exchange rate movements can lead to a gain in the competitive position of firms in one country at the expense of another, the timing of the business cycles may not always coincide, and in the longer term, countries may go through different phases of rapid or slow growth.

The BCG Approach

Before discussing recent, more sophisticated, versions of the portfolio approach, it is necessary to set out the basic features of the original analysis of the Boston Consulting Group (BCG), which has become widely known (although subject to increasing criticism) in recent years. The BCG approach, like its successors, revolves around a so-called *Directional Policy Matrix* (DPM), which is merely a way of classifying the different businesses by locating them on a two-dimensional grid. (Although portfolio analysis has become virtually synonymous with the use of such matrices, there is no inherent reason why it should be tied to this presentational device any more than is the financial analysis of a portfolio of stocks and shares.)

The original BCG approach was based on a classification of activities according to two characteristics: (a) the rate of growth of the industry of which it is part and (b) the market share of the company in question.[2] The relevance of industry growth is fairly straightforward. Rapid growth makes it easier for the individual firm to expand its activities by maintaining or increasing its market share, and hence provides profitable investment opportunities. Lack of growth makes it more difficult.

The second feature − emphasis on market share − is based on the thesis that, the higher a firm's market share in relation to its competitors, the stronger its competitive position. This is a more debatable proposition (see pp. 107−8). Clearly the achievement of a high market share is generally a consequence of a strong competitive position; but looking to the future, a current high market share may be the key to high profitability and future growth, but not necessarily. We shall return to this point later in this chapter and in the following chapter on Competitive Strategy.

The measure of market strength used by BCG is 'relative competitive position', as defined by 'relative market share': the market share of the business in question divided by that of the largest of its competitors. Thus, if the largest firm (A) has 50 per cent of the market and the next largest (B) has 25 per cent, A's relative market share will be 2 and B's will be ½.

The BCG matrix thus classifies business units or activities according to 'business growth rate' (by which they mean the growth of the market for the product) along the vertical axis, and relative competitive position or market share along the horizontal axis.

The well-known BCG growth-share matrix is divided into four quadrants, with businesses classified as 'Stars', 'Cash-Cows', 'Dogs' and 'Question Marks' (see figure 6.1).

Having established numerical values for growth rates and relative competitive position for the various activities within an enterprise, it is, of course, arbitrary where the break-points between high and low growth rates and between high and low market shares are set. As far as growth rates are concerned, the rate of growth of gross domestic product represents an obvious way of striking an average for growth rates in different industries and services. As far as relative competitive position is concerned, the BCG suggest a break-point at 1.5 (or 1.0 in low growth areas); this means that the firm in question must have a market share 1.5 times as great (or at least as great, where growth is slow) as that of the largest competitor apart from itself. Thus any firm which is not the market leader would be regarded as having a low 'relative competitive position'. Any suggestion that market leadership is essential to good profitability is, however, clearly false, and a gross oversimplification of the market determinants of profitability: for a statistical analysis of this see Michael Porter.[3]

A useful presentational device in drawing BCG and similar matrices is to indicate the size of the activity (e.g. as measured by sales or assets employed) by the area of the circle denoting its place on the grid (see figure 6.2).

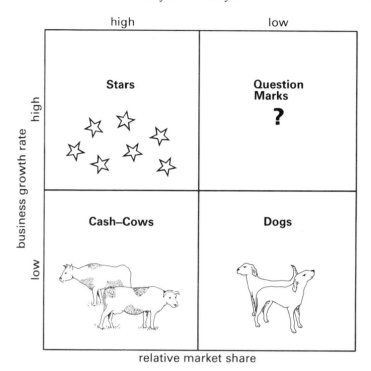

Figure 6.1 BCG matrix

Stars 'Stars' are businesses in the high-growth, high-share quadrant. Their key characteristics (according to the BCG) are that they are growing rapidly, use and generate large amounts of cash, and are frequently roughly in balance on cash flow. Stars present the best profit growth and investment opportunities, and every effort should be made to consolidate their position.

Cash-Cows 'Cash-Cows' are businesses with low growth but high market share. They should have an entrenched superior market position and low costs. Because of their low growth, their investment needs should be low and they should generate cash surpluses; in other words, they can be 'milked' for cash for the benefit of the rest of the corporation.

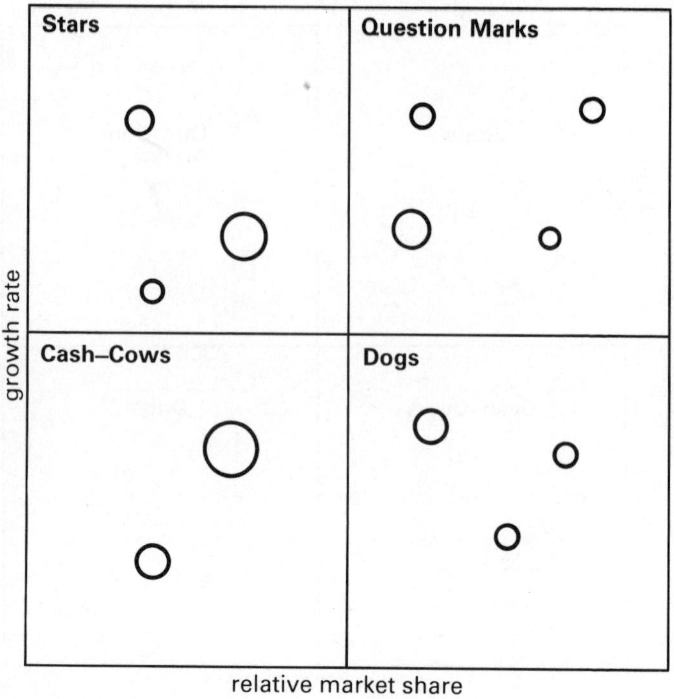

Figure 6.2 Graphical representation of portfolio. (The area of the circle is proportional to the size of the business, e.g. sales or assets.)

Dogs 'Dogs' are low-growth, low-share businesses. They are assumed to have low profits, and they may have a net cash requirement if investment is needed to keep them in business. They are candidates for liquidation.

Question marks 'Question marks' have a high growth rate and low market share. They are assumed to have high cash requirements for expansion but low cash generation because their low market share is equated to low profitability. They are called 'question marks' because they raise the question of whether money should be put into them to raise market share and hence profitability, or whether they should be dropped. (Again, the validity of this categorisation depends on the highly debatable contention that a small market share in a growth industry means poor profitability.)

Prescription for Strategy

Having classified individual activities in this way, the BCG prescription for manipulating the portfolio is as follows. The first goal should be to maintain the Cash-Cows without investing too much in them. The cash generated by the Cows should be used to consolidate the position of the Stars, and any surplus could be devoted to developing *some* of the Question Marks. The Dogs must be recognised as the weak point of the business and handled ruthlessly: they should be managed for cash, with minimal or no investment. Management should be wary of expensive 'turn-around' plans for the Dogs and must be prepared to liquidate them if necessary.

The progenitors of this approach see the classification of activities into these four categories as changing over the course of time. As growth in their industries slows down, the original Stars should become Cash-Cows, provided they maintain their high market share; if not, they will fall into the Dog category. A strong point of the BCG approach is the idea of classifying activities along these lines both today and in, say, five years' time, thus stimulating consideration both of the present pattern of the portfolio and also the directions in which it is likely to change if current strategies continue.

The weak points of the original BCG approach are the excessive reliance on market share as an indicator of competitive strength, and the assumption that profitability is consistently predictable from industry growth and market share. Subsequent developments of this approach have adopted more sophisticated ways both of assessing the attractiveness of the industry (as opposed to the simple measure of rate of growth) and of assessing the firm's competitive position; but they still focus attention on surrogates for profitability, rather than analysing the actual profitability of the activity and the factors determining it.

There are, nevertheless, a number of useful points in the

simple BCG approach. It emphasises the need to watch the contribution of each part of the business to the overall cash flow. The emphasis on the need to be selective rather than trying to reinforce activities all along the line is valuable, as is the ruthless attitude towards Dogs. It is always difficult to be sufficiently selective and ruthless in multi-divisional organisations where the top management tends to comprise the advocates and defenders of all the main activities. On the other hand, a fundamental weakness of this and similar approaches is that they completely neglect the human aspect and assume that central management is effectively divorced from the management of the individual business activities.

The PIMS Programme

The BCG emphasis on market share was supported by the Profit Impact of Market Strategy (PIMS) programme, which originated in General Electric and is now run by the Strategic Planning Institute. The staff of the Institute analyse data contributed confidentially by member companies to try to discover 'general "laws" that determine what business strategy in what kind of competitive environment produces what profit results'. Their conclusion was that profitability was closely linked to market share and that a 10-percentage-point improvement in market share was associated with a 5-percentage-point improvement in return on investment.[4] This, of course, begs the question of whether high market share was the cause of high profitability, or whether they were both due to common factors such as low costs and good management.

A number of possible explanations of the relationship were put forward. The first was the BCG's other leading 'product', the 'Experience Curve', which suggested that, each time the accumulated production of a product doubled, unit costs in real terms declined by a percentage, characteristically in the region of 20 to 30 per cent.[5]

Two other possible factors were that the large firm had greater market power, and that it could employ better-quality management. There was no evidence that the higher profit margins associated with higher market share reflected higher prices.

With the development of the PIMS programme and the growth of its data base, their analysis has tended to focus on a number of factors determining return on investment and other measures of profitability, with rather less emphasis on market share or relative market share on its own. They now attach particular importance to relative product and/or service quality as perceived by the customer and regard this as a key determinant of market share. The PIMS analysis now uses about two dozen 'strategic characteristics' which account for about 70 per cent of the variations in profitability among units in their database. Their other additional factors include: investment intensity, value added per employee, capacity utilisation, vertical integration, industry concentration. These findings are discussed in *The PIMS Principles* by Buzzell and Gale.[6]

BCG Second Thoughts

Over time, BCG have also modified their approach to take account of the fact that market share is not necessarily synonymous with competitive strength. In a series of articles in the *Financial Times* in November 1981, Michael Gould of the BCG maintained that it is valuable to be the market leader for branded goods, with the advantage of price leadership and the ability to spread marketing and distribution costs over a high volume; but economies of scale may be achieved even by a firm that is not the largest producer in the industry. Gould also made the point that the analysis of market share is highly dependent on the definition of what constitutes a product or activity within the firm and what constitutes the total market for it. A broad definition of market will give a lower market share than a narrower one; a firm that has a leading position in a specialist market may appear to have a low share in a more general market.

Gould, in his revision of the Boston doctrine, also changes the approach to the concept of market share by talking about regrouping products according to manufacturing process in order to reflect economies of scale in manufacturing rather than in market leadership. But other versions of the matrix approach have already gone much further than Boston in providing an analytical framework which allows a wider array of factors to be taken into account.

Matrix Approach Developments

The basic approach of analysing business units or products according to (a) the characteristics of the market sector in question and (b) the competitive position of the unit or product has been developed to derive an assessment of these two measures by combining a number of factors in each case. These developments are associated with the use of the DPM by General Electric, McKinsey and Shell. Their characteristic matrix is shown in figure 6.3. Thus, instead of equating *market attractiveness* with the rate of growth of sales of the product, the future profitability of the sector can be assessed in terms of the main factors believed to influence it — not only the rate of growth of sales, but also the nature of the competition, including the pricing policy of the market leaders, entry conditions, vulnerability to foreign competitors, prospects of new technology and new products and, where possible the analysis of the financial results of companies in this field. In other words, the input to the matrix becomes a thorough environmental assessment, rather than using market growth as a proxy for all the factors determining sector profitability.

Similarly, *competitive position* can be analysed in terms not only of market share, but also of product quality, service, distribution arrangements, plant capacity and characteristics, ability to develop new products, etc. — in effect, any of the factors which would be examined in an assessment of the firm's strengths and weaknesses in the market (see also chapter 7).

To present the results of such an analysis in matrix form, it is necessary to give (a) each sector and (b) each business a score or number of marks for each factor; then, by weighting the factors, it is possible to derive a total score for the profitability of that sector. The factors considered worth examination, the method of scoring and the weights adopted can all be chosen to suit the firm and the exercise

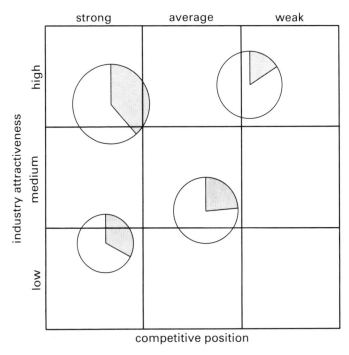

Figure 6.3　GE business screen. (The area of the circle denotes the size of the industry; the shaded portion represents market share.)

in hand; it is, however, essential that they should be agreed and understood by all the participants. An example of such a scoring system is given in tables 6.1 and 6.2.

A further refinement of the matrix approach is the *Risk Matrix* developed by Harbridge House.[7] This approach takes ten to fifteen key issues such as inflation, exchange rate changes, expropriation, etc. It then assesses (a) the impact on profits if such a development occurs and (b) the probability that it will occur. The severity of the impact on profits is graded from, say, 1 to 6 and multiplied by the probability. Thus a further matrix can be produced showing market prospects on one axis and environmental risk on the other. For those prepared to work in more than two dimensions, this can be combined with the market growth/

TABLE 6.1 Industry Attractiveness:
Specimen Scoring System

Criteria	Weight	Rating (1 to 5)	Score
Size of market	0.10	4	0.40
Growth rate	0.20	3	0.60
Competitive structure and pricing policy	0.15	3	0.45
Profitability	0.40	4	1.60
Technology	0.10	2	0.20
Social factors	0.05	3	0.15
Total	1.00		3.40 (maximum 5)

TABLE 6.2 Competitive Position:
Specimen Scoring System

Criteria	Weight	Rating (1 to 5)	Score
Growth rate	0.10	5	0.50
Market share	0.10	3	0.30
Strategic position	0.10	4	0.40
Profitability	0.20	3	0.60
Technology	0.15	3	0.45
Location	0.10	2	0.20
Management	0.10	3	0.30
Workforce	0.10	3	0.30
Corporate image	0.05	5	0.25
Total	1.00		3.30 (maximum 5)

competitive strength matrix to form a three-dimensional matrix!

It is important to avoid confusion between the use of

Directional Policy Matrices as essentially a useful presentational device (with all the dangers of oversimplification) and the fundamental work of analysing the prospects for the market sectors and products under review and the present and future competitive position of the firm's own business unit or product.

Portfolio Objectives

The action to be taken in the light of any such portfolio analysis must reflect the four basic objectives of the managers of the portfolio. The first is that so far as possible, each unit should be good of its kind, that is, in a strong competitive position and profitable. This objective may not always be achieved, but it does not require any elaborate analysis to point to the problem of loss-makers.

The second major objective, as explained at the beginning of this chapter, is to achieve a balance of cash generation and requirements which matches the overall financial strategy of the enterprise. This does not necessarily mean a balanced cash flow with no net borrowing or generation of cash reserves. It does mean that the overall cash position is under control and that borrowing requirements and periodic access to the market follow a perceived corporate financial strategy. The firm may be thrown off course in the short term if there are too many 'Question Marks' which lead to inadequate cash flow and profitability. It may suffer in the longer term if it is too highly dependent on short-term profit producers without developing sufficient long-term growth prospects. On the other hand, trying to run too many promising developers at once may lead to excessive cash demands and an unstable growth of profits, leading to a lack of market confidence.

For the firm to achieve the third objective of corporate 'immortality', while its component businesses or products flourish and then die, it needs a balance of new, mature and dying businesses or products. Diversity in this sense (which may be achieved within a single industry) is often of more fundamental importance to a healthy business than diversity in the sense of a spread over different industries or products, although the fourth objective — reducing financial risk — may encourage wider diversification of the portfolio.

Gap-closing

The gap-closing approach outlined in chapter 2 can be applied to the problem of getting the right portfolio. Starting with an analysis of the present portfolio, the next step is to consider what it may look like in, say, five years' time with a continuation of the firm's present investment policies. This forecast portfolio should then be compared with what might be regarded as the target portfolio, and options identified for closing the gap. The key measures for doing so are, first, what might be regarded as 'pure' portfolio management, namely, buying or selling businesses. The second line of attack is for corporate management to change the pattern of development between its different component businesses, by altering the allocation of investment funds. Finally, there is the possibility of corporate action to improve the management and efficiency of the businesses themselves.

The Role of Portfolio Analysis

Portfolio analysis is a tool for formulating business at corporate level, looking at the corporation as a collection of investments in different businesses, as distinct from an analysis at individual business level. This distinction is made most clearly by Hofer and Schendel in what is probably the most effective exposition of this approach in its proper perspective.[8] Portfolio analysis is most applicable to the true conglomerate business with a collection of unrelated activities and to situations where market, rather than supply, factors are predominant. There is no necessary reason why portfolio analysis should be equated solely with matrix analysis; indeed, the latter is no substitute for a thorough analysis of profitability and cash flow.

Finally, it is important to remember that running a conglomerate is not the same as managing a financial portfolio. Buying and selling companies is not the same as buying and selling shares. The human implications for managers and workers cannot be ignored. Corporate management has to consider the impact of changes in ownership on the management of the companies involved. Moreover, the top management of the subsidiaries may in effect be regarded as members of the corporate management team, thus creating serious difficulties and resistance to divestment.

It is bound to be difficult to motivate management in the subsidiaries if corporate or portfolio objectives conflict with the natural objectives of those working in the subsidiary — for example, if corporate management wants to milk it for short-term profit or run it into the ground. Devolution of management within a conglomerate requires a certain expectation that each unit will run itself as efficiently as possible and that the incentive to do so will not be destroyed by denial of funds for investment to exploit business opportunities.

As far as the workers in the subsidiaries are concerned, they will react strongly against changes of ownership that threaten their security and livelihood.

In summary, the portfolio approach can provide a useful analytical tool for approaching the strategy problems of diversified companies, but it does not generate any new ventures or options, and it ignores the crucial relationships between new and existing activities discussed in chapter 5. The basic managerial problems experienced in integrated firms must still bulk large in the corporate strategy of any large organisation, however limited its degree of integration. The weakness of the portfolio approach is that it puts all the emphasis on what businesses you own, rather than what you do with them.

Notes

1 For a discussion of the relation between Portfolio Analysis and the Product Life Cycle, see Hiram C. Barksdale and

Clyde E. Harris, Jr, 'Portfolio Analysis and the Product Life Cycle', *Long Range Planning Journal*, December 1982.

2 Barry Hedley, 'Strategy and the Business Portfolio', *Long Range Planning*, February 1977.

3 Michael E. Porter, *Competitive Strategy*, 1980, chapter 7, and 'The Structure within Industries and Companies' Performance', *Review of Economics and Statistics*, May 1979.

4 R. D. Buzzell, B. T. Gale and R. G. M. Sultan, 'Market Share − A Key to Profitability', *Harvard Business Review*, January−February 1975.

5 Barry Hedley, 'A Fundamental Approach to Strategy Development', *Long Range Planning*, December 1976.

6 R. D. Buzzell and B. T. Gale, *The PIMS Principles − Linking Strategy to Performance*, 1987. These later results still indicate that a 5 point rise in ROI is associated with a 10 point rise in (relative) market share. See also: B. T. Gale and Ben Branch, '"Allocating" Capital More Effectively', *Sloane Management Review*, Fall 1987.

7 David E. Hussey, *Introducing Corporate Planning* (2nd edn), 1979, chapter 8.

8 Charles W. Hofer and Dan Schendel, *Strategy Formulation: Analytical Concepts*, 1978.

7
Competitive Strategy

Competitive strategy is that aspect of strategy which is concerned with how to do better than your competitors. Rumelt has described it as 'the art of creating or exploiting those advantages that are most telling, enduring and most difficult to duplicate'.[1] He attributes competitive advantage to one of three roots: superior resources, superior skills or superior position. The idea of 'positional' advantage is familiar in military strategy, chess or diplomacy. In business, positional advantage reflects such factors as a well-established position in the market, economies of scale or technical leadership − advantages that may be as important in deterring competitors as in beating them. To quote the earliest known guide to strategy, *The Art of War* by Sun Tzu, written over two thousand years ago, 'To subdue the enemy without fighting is the acme of skill.'[2]

The concept of competitive strategy has been developed in greatest depth by Michael Porter in his book of that name, and its sequel *Competitive Advantage*.[3] He emphasises the importance of analysing the nature of the competition and market structure in the industry in question and the likely reactions of competitors to a firm's strategic moves. This chapter is largely based on his work. The approach is relevant both to Strategic Business Units within a diversified enterprise and to the Corporation as a whole when it is operating mainly within one industry.

Structural Analysis

The economist tends to assume that competition in the market place and competition to secure finance will equalise returns on investment in different industries 'at the margin'. The business strategist, on the other hand, is pre-occupied with the visible differences in returns in different activities and hence the possibilities of securing more than average returns. Porter seeks to explain differences in re-turns between industries in terms of five factors leading to divergences from the economist's classical concept of free competition. These are:

1 barriers to entry (and exit);
2 the degree of competition among existing firms;
3 pressure from substitute products;
4 the bargaining power of buyers;
5 the bargaining power of suppliers.

Barriers to Entry

Where there are a number of factors that make it difficult or expensive for newcomers to enter an industry (*barriers to entry*), the level of profitability in that industry will tend to be higher than average. Porter identifies six main barriers to entry:

1 **Economies of scale**, either in production, distribution, or research and development. The automobile industry is an obvious example.
2 **Product differentiation**: building up a new brand name may be very expensive.
3 **Switching costs**: buyers may have to scrap existing equip-ment or methods of operation to use a new product.
4 **Access to distribution channels**: the newcomer must persuade, or provide an incentive to, the distributor to handle the product before he can reach the final customer.
5 **Cost advantages of established producers**: this may con-sist of established 'know-how', partly written-off capital assets, or access to components, materials or labour.
6 **Government regulation or licensing** may protect exist-ing producers.

The other major obstacle to entry may be the threat of retaliation by existing producers. A correct assessment of this threat may be essential to survival. It depends on the size and financial strength of existing firms and the extent to which the entry of a newcomer threatens their profitability. Existing producers are much more sensitive to a threat to existing price levels than to losing market share. Hence newcomers whose potential volume is quite small may still be regarded as a major threat if their activities are likely to bring down existing price levels.

Barriers to Exit

The converse of barriers to entry is *barriers to exit*. These are the factors that deter firms from moving out of unprofitable industries and make it harder to eliminate surplus capacity. They comprise such obstacles as the lack of any market for the assets employed (e.g. redundant steelworks), the fact that the products in question may share production facilities with other more profitable products, and the desire to satisfy customers by maintaining a wide range of products.[4]

The existence of such obstacles to moving out of particular lines of business tends to accentuate the tendency to cut-throat competition, price-cutting and low (or negative) profitability.

Competition

The degree of competition depends partly on the number and relative size of the firms in the industry. A fragmented industry with a large number of small firms tends to be very competitive. The situation in an industry concentrated in the hands of a few firms may depend on whether there is a clear leader and if so on its pricing policy. Competition among a few large firms of more or less equal strength may create an unstable situation.

Factors making for intense competition are slow industry growth, high fixed costs, commodity-type products which are difficult to differentiate, and additions to capacity which have to come in large increments: all factors endemic in the steel industry, for cxample. Competition will also be intense where the firms are playing for high strategic stakes (such as recognition by government as the leading supplier) and where exit barriers are high.

The existence of substitute products will tend to act as a further competitive factor limiting profits.

Bargaining Power of Buyers and Suppliers

The bargaining power of buyers may be an important factor affecting profitability. Where there are only a few powerful buyers, competing fiercely among themselves (as in the automobile industry), they may be in a very strong position *vis-à-vis* their component suppliers. Conversely, a fragmented industry supplied by one or two large firms may be in a weak position (for example the building industry as compared with cement producers).

Strategic Groups

The various firms within an industry are likely to follow a number of different strategies, but they can be divided into groups of firms, each of which is following broadly similar strategies. In the automobile industry, Ford and General Motors might be classified as part of a 'strategic group' consisting of global producers with a full product line; at the other extreme, Rolls Royce and Jaguar are producing for a specialised segment of the market with limited production facilities. Formulating a competitive strategy can be viewed as deciding which strategic group to join, or whether indeed to create a new group.

The concept of barriers to entry to an industry may be extended to barriers to mobility within an industry; in other words, the costs that a firm would incur by shifting from one strategic group to another (for example, Rolls Royce attempting to cover a broad product range, or General Motors competing at the top of the quality range). By limiting the ability of firms to move from one group to another, such barriers or costs provide a measure of protection to groups with higher than average profitability.

The way in which an industry is divided into strategic groups may have an important bearing on the degree of competition in the industry. If different strategic groups are selling similar products to the same customers, competition will be intense. An example is the competition between 'mini-steel works' and the major integrated producers. They each follow different strategies: the former have small, scrap-based, electric arc works with simplified management structures; the latter have one or more large works with a divisionalised management structure. But on the products they both produce, competition is intense. On the other hand, where the difference in strategies involves selling different products or meeting the needs of different customers, competition between strategic groups is minimised.

The profitability of the individual firm depends not only on the industry and the strategic group within that industry, but also on its position within the strategic group. Where there are significant economies of scale, its size within the group may affect its production or selling costs, or its capability to develop new products. There is, however, no simple relationship between profitability and market share.

Market Share

Porter's own work suggests that

> the relationship between the profitability of larger and smaller market shares depends on the industry. . . . followers were noticeably more profitable than leaders in 15 of 38 industries. The industries in which the followers' rates of return were higher appear generally to be those where economies of scale are either not great or absent (clothing, footwear, pottery, meat products, carpets) and/or those that are highly segmented (optical, medical, ophthalmic goods, liquor, periodicals, carpets, and toys and sporting goods). The industries in which leaders' rates of return are higher seem to be generally those with heavy advertising (soap, perfumes, soft drinks, grain mill products, i.e. cereal, cutlery) and/or research outlays and production economies of scale (radio and television, drugs, photographic equipment). This outcome is as we would expect.[5]

Further studies by Woo of firms with (a) low market shares and high profitability and (b) high market shares and low profitability show parallel results.[6] Relatively profitable low-share firms were involved in 'the sale of standardised industrial components and supplies without the provision of a particularly high level of custom features or auxiliary services...characterised by high purchase frequency, high value added and large number of competitors'. Such firms went in for intense marketing, high product value and careful cost control, whereas the less successful low-share companies tended to ape their larger competitors with broad product lines and expensive R and D activities. Market leaders with low returns were located in slowly growing fragmented markets. Their products were older and tended to have a lower value added. Woo concludes that the benefits of both high and low market shares depend on a host of factors such as the characteristics of the market, the product, the organisation of the firm and its competitive strategy.

Successful Strategies

What, then, are the essentials for a successful and profitable competitive strategy? Porter categorises successful strategies as involving one or more of three elements:

1 cost leadership;
2 product differentiation;
3 specialisation by focusing on a particular market segment.

Achieving the lowest costs in the industry is frequently dependent on also reaching a high enough volume of sales to exploit the available economies of scale. So it tends to be a strategy associated with an aggressive sales policy and a fairly extensive product range. Product differentiation, on the other hand, is aimed at securing higher profit margins by making customers less sensitive to price. The third strategy of specialisation is designed to ensure that everything the company does is done well, whether it be, say, customer service or product design, because the firm is concentrating on particular needs to which it is better tuned than any of its competitors.

Low profitability is frequently associated with failure to

develop in any one of these three directions and hence become 'stuck in the middle'. A firm with indifferent costs, no distinct product features to differentiate itself from its competitors, and specialising in no particular area of the market needs to make a fundamental strategic decision to move in at least one of these three directions.

The experience of the Burton Group of clothing manufacturers and retailers in the UK provides striking examples of both success and failure. Starting with one shop in 1901, Montague Burton had created an empire of over 600 branches when he died in 1952. His success was based on specialisation in the market for low-priced, made-to-measure men's suits and introducing economies of scale into a traditionally back-room process. But as the market for made-to-measure suits declined, Burton became an example of the dangers of failure to readjust quickly enough to changing conditions, in this case by retuning its products and outlets to the growing trend towards more casual styles of clothes. In the early 1970s Burton started to try to adapt its products to meet the needs of different segments of the market. Maintaining its existing chain of shops, the firm began to offer three different product ranges: one catering for the executive end of the market, one for the middle-of-the-road and one for the young and trendy. It continued, however, to sell them all from its existing shops, and depended heavily on its own manufacturing capacity. The results were disappointing. 'Burton's fundamental problem lay in its failure to segment the menswear market. It attempted to be all things to all men, and as a result failed to develop any one product group for any group of customers.'[7]

In the field of women's clothing, on the other hand, where Burton introduced Top Shops into the Peter Robinson chain — trendy shops within a shop — these were more successful. This recipe was later followed by the introduction of Top Man shops catering for a similar age group. By 1978 there were 44 of these and Burton had virtually halved the number of its traditional men's shops. It had also drastically cut its manufacturing capacity, relying on outside purchases to meet a growing proportion of its requirements. As a result, the losses of the mid-1970s were turned into substantial profits.

Strategies for Different Types of Industries

Chapter 1 emphasised the extent to which the nature of the strategy problems facing a firm depended on the industry in which it was operating, with particular reference to such distinctive characteristics as resulted from the nature of its markets and its products, and its technology of production. Porter discusses the common elements of strategy in five main types of industry:

1 fragmented;
2 emerging;
3 in transition to maturity;
4 declining;
5 global.

Fragmented Industries

'Fragmented' industries consist of a large number of relatively small businesses, for example retailing, building and many sectors of engineering. From time to time opportunities may occur to build up large organisations in such industries, which secure definite advantages of scale (for example, department and chain stores in retailing), but these are comparatively rare. More often it is necessary to find ways of living profitably in an industry inevitably populated by small-scale enterprises. There may, however, be ways of securing advantages of scale while leaving individual operational units to operate on a small scale. Franchising may secure economies of scale where individually owned shops benefit from common advertising or the large-scale supply of materials and equipment – for example, the Prontaprint shops offering office printing and copying services. The Happy Eater and Little Chef chains of roadside cafes in the UK are cases where establishing a national brand image and catering for a specialist segment of the market (the motorist) has been a successful formula for large-scale competition in a highly fragmented field.

A recipe for failure is trying to dominate such an industry by operating on a large scale where there are many disadvantages and few advantages in doing so. Unless large company overheads bring definite advantages in competing with small-scale producers, they will merely result in excessive costs. Centralisation is a similar pitfall in industries where local contacts and quick service are the keynote to success.

Emerging Industries

'The essential characteristic of an emerging industry from the viewpoint of formulating strategy is that there are no rules of the game.'[8] New industries face the strategist with the highest degree of uncertainty, but also the greatest number of degrees of freedom within which to act. In considering whether to enter a new industry, the key question to be faced is not whether the industry will grow rapidly, but how profitable it will prove to be in the long run.

In a new industry, one of the major tasks of the firms, individually and collectively, is to establish the industry and its products in the eyes of potential customers. Thus, one strategic issue is how far to go it alone in developing markets and how far to co-operate with other firms in publicising new products and their possible uses, and generally establishing the reputation of the new industry.

New industries are generally started by one or two pioneers while others stand on the sidelines trying to decide at what point to enter the game, hoping someone else will make the initial mistakes. This applies particularly to the larger company, which tends to enter after it is clear that the industry is going to take off successfully. Fortunately for the economy, the pioneers are frequently motivated by vision and faith as much as by nicely balanced calculation, or they might be deterred by the danger of the returns on their initial expenditure being threatened as competitors with greater resources moved into the field. On the other hand, the successful pioneer may establish a name and reputation virtually synonymous with the product — just as for years the word 'Hoover' was generally used as a generic term for vacuum cleaner.

Maturing Industries

The transition to maturity in an industry often creates a new situation for firms within it and precipitates the need for rethinking their strategies. As sales grow more slowly, there is increasing competition for market share. This may take the form of increasing competition in either service or price. Over-capacity may emerge as firms are slow to adjust to slower growth in demand. The pace of development of new products and applications slackens. International competition sharpens. Profits are harder to come by.

In such a situation it may become essential for the firm to redefine its strategy and make a definite choice of direction. In this phase of management, increased emphasis on financial control becomes important, and with it sophisticated cost analysis as a basis for decisions on product mix and price structure. Increased emphasis on reducing manufacturing costs may shift the emphasis from product innovation to developing processes or simplifying product design to improve production costs. The new style of management requires greater emphasis on quantitative long-term planning and the introduction of regular planning machinery.

Porter's three basic types of strategy (cost leadership, product differentiation and market specialisation) each provides a possible strategic answer to be considered in the light of a realistic assessment of the strengths and weaknesses of the firm. At this stage the danger of over-optimism or self-delusion based on the previous experience of rapid growth can be serious. Common pitfalls are failing to acknowledge the need to be more competitive on price; banking on the further development of new products instead of competing successfully with existing products; and continuing to allow excess capacity to develop.

Declining Industries

For some years, the only guidance on strategy in declining industries was that provided by the exponents of the portfolio approach, which was in effect: 'make what money you can [harvest], and then get out [divest] and leave it to someone else.' This advice was based on a simple view of the inevitability of the 'product life cycle', although products (unlike human beings) do not necessarily ever die. This may have been helpful to the top management of large conglomerates in devising their corporate strategies. It was no help to the wretched manager trying to run the unit in question, or the host of independent companies in the declining industry. Nor did it in practice face up to the human problems of deliberately and cynically running down part of a large business without a total collapse of morale in the management and labour force. Moreover the much heralded strategy of divestment presupposes that there is a market for lame ducks at any price, which there frequently is not. Often in such cases their most significant asset is the value of their order book to a close competitor, but where this does not seem attractive their other assets may be unsaleable.

Recently, greater attention has been paid to strategies for declining industries.[9] The first essential is to study the reasons for the decline in demand and the characteristics of the remaining market. Is the existing product being replaced by a newly developing product which will eventually take over the whole market − or is the new product merely another competitor that will exist alongside the existing product (e.g. petrol and electric lawn mowers)? Are changing social patterns leading to the extinction of demand for such a product or service (e.g. domestic laundry)? Is the fall in demand a temporary phenomenon reflecting a particular set of economic circumstances or government policies (e.g. cuts in public investment)? In particular, when there is general economic depression it is difficult to differentiate between a secular decline in an industry and the effects of current macroeconomic conditions. The fact that demand for a particular industry may have fallen more than average may not be a sign of a long-term decline, but rather of the industry's sensitivity to cyclical conditions; for example, capital goods industries may be particularly badly hit by a recession, or export industries by a temporary rise in the exchange rate.

Where the industry is in secular decline, which segments of the market are likely to be the first to go? Will potentially profitable niches be left, such as servicing existing equipment or selling replacement parts? Will costly exit barriers keep other firms active in an increasingly unprofitable market? The difficulty in answering these questions, and hence the uncertainty about the industry's future, is a major factor inhibiting the development of appropriate strategies in such industries.

Harrigan postulates two dimensions in which one can measure the extent to which the firm remains committed to a declining industry. The first is its market share; the second is its level of investment. On this basis she distinguishes five types of strategy:

1 increasing investment in order to seek dominance;
2 holding investment steady;
3 shrinking selectively;
4 harvesting or milking for immediate profit;
5 divesting now.

Porter has a broadly similar grouping, but substituting for the first three just two categories:

1 seeking leadership;
2 finding a profitable niche.

It is perhaps inevitable in a declining industry that all these types of strategy carry serious risks of losing money. Seeking leadership is only worthwhile if the industry is likely to be profitable after rationalisation and if the cost of investing in new plant or buying up other companies or their assets is not excessive. The intermediate strategy of holding investment steady and consolidating what one conceives to be the more robust parts of the business can be solely a rationale for not facing up to the extent of the decline. Looking for a profitable niche is in many ways the most promising approach for the average firm, in that it concentrates attention on the nature of the changes taking place in the market, and the change in stance required of the firm to adjust to them. Harvesting and divesting, as already said, are easier to conceive than to execute.

Global Industries

A 'global' corporation (in Porter's terms) is a multinational whose competitive position in different countries is interrelated, as distinct from one with autonomous subsidiaries in different countries whose operations are largely independent. This interrelationship generally reflects the sale of common (or closely related) products in many national markets — as with aircraft, computers or copiers. The evolution of global firms tends to reflect economies of scale, mainly in production or research and development, and thus it is natural that so many should have been nurtured in the United States, and now Japan, with large national markets.

The strategic alternatives available to such firms in marketing terms are broadly similar to those operating on a national basis. They have to decide whether to market a full range of products across a wide geographical area, or to focus on particular market segments in terms of products or countries.

An important additional dimension is the intervention of national governments to support the home based competitor, by trade or financial measures, or through public sector purchasing policies. The relationship between production costs and selling prices is also continually shifting as exchange rates vary. Both these factors create pressures to invest in production facilities in major markets rather than to rely too heavily on concentration of production in any one country — however great the theoretical economies of scale.

One of the key strategic weapons used by such firms is the creation of alliances or joint ventures, particularly with indigenous firms in potentially valuable markets. Such potential allies may be valuable because they have well-established products or markets. They can also be valuable if they are weak, but the government concerned is anxious to maintain or establish production facilities in the industry, and foreign investment and technical co-operation provide a means of doing so. Japanese investment in the UK car industry and American investment in high technology industry in Scotland are good examples.

Defensive and Offensive Strategies

Porter has developed a number of guidelines for formulating 'defensive' or 'offensive' strategies: this is perhaps the nearest business strategy gets to a direct analogy with

Competitive Strategy

military strategy.[10] The first line of defence must be to reduce so far as possible any potential new entrant's or competitor's expectation of the gains to be achieved. This is akin to making any barriers to entry as high as possible. Very often such moves will take the form of increasing the scale of operation needed to succeed (e.g. increasing advertising expenditure), providing extensive service coverage, or widening the product range. Other devices include measures to tie retailers or customers more firmly to their existing supplier.

The second line of defence is to signal clearly to the would-be aggressor that he will meet a determined response (i.e. deterrence is the best defence). Statements about a firms's intention to maintain its market share or increase capacity may influence the boards of its competitors. Most effective are actions which visibly demonstrate its determination and ability to respond. The creation of new capacity somewhat ahead of demand is one tactic, albeit a potentially costly one that needs to be treated with caution. Reacting sharply in terms of price-cutting and sales effort to any incursion into its prime markets is another. In my time in the steel industry this was a well-established custom: a producer would react to any undercutting by foreign firms in its home market by selling a corresponding tonnage at low prices in the rival's own home market in order to fire a warning shot across his bows. This illustrates the need to take a long-term strategic view in making such a response, and not being inhibited by considerations of short-term profitability.

In deciding on defensive tactics, one obvious basic consideration should be to adopt, so far as possible, measures which increase the value of the firm's products to the buyer, thus strengthening both its short-term and long-term position in the market.

Devising successful policies to pre-empt or ward off attack depends on a realistic appreciation both of the structure of the industry and of the objectives and strengths of a possible competitor. What is it trying to achieve? How important is the foray into new territory to its underlying strategy? Does it need the sales to fill capacity or complement existing product lines, or is it just looking for additional profitable business? An appreciation of how important success is to the attacker may be a key factor in determining the best response, in particular whether to stand and fight or beat a tactical retreat.

When it comes to offensive strategy, Porter's cardinal rule 'is not to attack head-on with an imitative strategy, regardless of the challenger's resources or staying power'. An attacker needs a different strategy. It must seek a sustainable competitive advantage either in cost or product quality, service or distribution facilities: for example, Timex stole a march on established watch producers by selling watches through drug stores and other mass retail outlets rather than through jewellers. The would-be attacker must then consider whether it can bear or thwart any potential retaliation − cf. Laker's defeat (chapter 1). In assessing potential reaction it is worth remembering that a very powerful, near monopolist, may not be able to retaliate as drastically as might seem possible at first sight because any such action might provoke public or government reaction, such as restrictive practice hearings.

An effective way of outflanking existing producers is to focus on a particular segment of the market and redefine its needs. David Robinson's development of TV rental as opposed to outright sales might be regarded as a highly successful example of such an approach.

Turnaround Strategies

A decline in demand for the industry's products (whether it be a permanent, long-term decline in sales or a temporary recession) is but one of many reasons why a firm may be in financial difficulties. Over-expansion, misplaced diversification, an inappropriate choice of products and markets, high production costs or inefficient operations (among other causes) may also get a firm into trouble. Strategies designed to cope with this type of situation have come to be known as *turnaround strategies*.

The dominating feature of turnaround situations is

generally shortage of time — the worse the financial situation, the shorter the time available to put it right. Initially, at any rate, the time available for analysis before decisions have to be taken is strictly limited and the immediate planning horizon is a matter of months rather than years. Drawing on his own experience of turnaround management in the United States, Bibeault distinguished three phases in the turnaround process.[11] Stage 1 is to get out an emergency plan to establish a positive cash flow. Stage 2 (lasting perhaps a year) is a stabilisation plan to ensure that this position is maintained. Stage 3 is a plan to return to growth over a period of, typically, up to three years. Slatter, who has studied successful turnaround management in a number of UK companies, makes a broadly similar distinction, dividing the process into four overlapping phases of: analysis; emergency action; strategic change; and growth.[12]

There are two basic types of problem to be dealt with: the operational and the strategic. The first arises from weaknesses in the day-to-day running of the company. The second reflects the need to adopt strategies which will make it possible for the company to recover. The two may, of course, be connected, in that, for example, a change in strategy is needed to get the company out of operating in fields where it is bound to be uncompetitive, or where fundamental changes in organisation or manpower policy are required. We are concerned here with the changes in strategy needed to turn round the company.

In a diversified company, the first essential is to identify which parts of the business are profitable (or have a reasonable chance of being made profitable) and which are not. The second step is to consider the cash requirements of the profitable businesses with development potential in relation to the cash flow of the company as a whole. The usual portfolio analysis approach (discussed in chapter 6) of relating the cash requirements of individual businesses to the overall financial position has to be interpreted very stringently in a company which has recently escaped from the threat of bankruptcy. It may be particularly important to limit the number of new developments in order not to spread any available funds too thinly.

Since the fact that the situation has got so bad is generally a sign of management weakness, a key question that must be raised is the ability of management to cope with the demands of all its peripheral activities. 'Over-diversification takes place when the management of a company cannot test the quantitative and qualitative information coming from a subsidiary against its experience.'[13] Some would argue that control by financial results alone has proved successful. But almost by definition, if the subsidiaries are showing persistently poor financial results, financial control alone has proved ineffective; if, then, central management are not in a position to get to grips with the underlying problems, they have lost control. This is one of the reasons why the results of unrelated diversification are often disappointing.

Disposal of diversified assets is frequently part of a turn-around strategy, either because they have failed to come up to expectations and have proved a distraction from running the core business successfully, or merely because they can be sold off to raise cash, whereas the core business is more or less indivisible. Slatter found that divestment took place in about one-half of all successful turnarounds.[14]

Thus, an emergency assessment of the firm's 'portfolio' of businesses is an essential aspect of turning round a diversified company. The second aspect (which applies whatever the degree of diversification) is to formulate strategies that will enable the business (or its component parts) to compete successfully again. In this task what has been said above about evolving successful competitive strategies is in most cases of critical importance; although, in addition to lack of an adequate competitive strategy, in the more limited sense, there may be basic operational weaknesses in financial control, sales and production management, etc.

The distinctive features of the turnaround situation are the need for speed and clear evidence that the existing strategic approach has failed. The ease or difficulty with which a more successful strategy can be evolved depends, then, partly on the circumstances of the industry, and is likely to be more difficult in a declining industry than an expanding one.

Notes

1 Richard P. Rumelt, 'The Evaluation of Business Strategy', in Lawrence R. Jauch and William F. Glueck, *Business Policy and Strategic Management*, 1980.
2 Samuel B. Griffith, *Sun Tzu: The Art of War*, 1963.
3 Michael E. Porter, *Competitive Strategy*, 1980 and *Competitive Advantage*, 1985.
4 See K. R. Harrigan, 'The Effect of Exit Barriers Upon Strategic Flexibility', *Strategic Management Journal*, April–June 1980.
5 Porter, *Competitive Strategy*, pp. 147, 148.
6 Caroline Y. Woo and Arnold C. Cooper, 'Strategies of Effective Low Share Businesses', *Strategic Management Journal*, July–September 1981; Caroline Y. Woo, 'Evaluation of the Strategies and Performance of Low ROI Market Share Leaders', *Strategic Management Journal*, April–June 1983.
7 Stuart Slatter, *Corporate Recovery: Successful Turnaround Strategies and their Implementation*, 1984.
8 Porter, *Competitive Strategy*.
9 K. R. Harrigan, *Strategies for Declining Industries*, 1980 (based on research into end-game strategies in seven industries); and Porter, *Competitive Strategy*.
10 Porter, *Competitive Advantage*, chapters 14 and 15.
11 Donald B. Bibeault, *Corporate Turnaround: How Managers Turn Losers into Winners*, 1982.
12 Slatter, *Corporate Recovery*.
13 Bibeault, *Corporate Turnaround*.
14 Slatter, *Corporate Recovery*.

8

Strategic Planning

Planning is one of the most complex and difficult
intellectual activities in which man can engage.
Not to do it well is not a sin, but to settle for
doing it less than well is.

Russell L. Ackoff.[1]

Planning, in the broadest sense of deciding in advance what
you intend to do and how you intend to do it, is not, of
course, just a business activity. As with strategy, it has its
origins in military operations, which have for centuries
been the most complex and large-scale operations that man
has tried to manage; and, to quote the military theorist and
historian, Liddell Hart, 'strategy depends for success, first
and most, on a sound calculation and co-ordination of the
end and the means.'[2] Indeed, even in recent years many of
the quantitative techniques now used in business planning
were originally developed in connection with military planning in the Second World War. Going beyond both the
business and military fields, perhaps the most demanding
feat of planning has been that required by NASA for such
feats as landing a man on the moon or developing the space
shuttle.[3]

This chapter is concerned with the development of planning in business, in particular long-term or strategic planning
as opposed to short-term operational planning. The distinction between a 'strategy' and a 'plan' is not a hard-and-fast
one, and different firms and writers distinguish between
them in different ways. The essential difference is that a
'strategy' is a broad statement of objectives and the policy
for achieving them, whereas a 'plan' is a more detailed and
quantitative statement both of objectives and means: it is
the first step in implementing the strategy. One of the

important practical consequences of this distinction is that the broad strategy of the enterprise should need less frequent revision than its more detailed long-term plans. For example, the strategy may be to acquire manufacturing facilities in North America; the plan would be concerned with their capacity, location, timing, costs, etc. The strategy would remain valid for years — indeed, unless it does it will prove disastrous. But the detailed plans will need to be revised as demand forecasts, production costs and so on evolve. The formulation or reformulation of strategy need not, and generally does not, take place at regular intervals; it depends how rapidly the situation changes. The preparation of plans, on the other hand, should so far as possible be one of the management activities conducted on a regular annual basis. Long-term plans are generally revised and rolled forward each year; they will cover, say, 1990–4 one year and 1991–5 the next.

Corporate Planning

The terms 'long-range planning', 'corporate planning' and 'strategic planning' are not strictly interchangeable, but in practice all tend to be used to cover much the same type of activity. The meaning of long-range and strategic as opposed to short-term or operational is clear; the concept of 'corporate' planning may need further explanation. It is used first to denote planning for the future of the organisation as a whole, and second planning for all aspects of the organisation's activities, as opposed to one limited function such as production or personnel. Since money is the common denominator and we are dealing with business organisations, corporate planning is necessarily heavily orientated towards the financial dimension.

Corporate planning has tended to evolve in two ways. The first is in order to elaborate the means of achieving strategic objectives; the second is as a development from physical or other forms of planning, for example, from forecasting long-term demand and capacity requirements. Where planning has been almost non-existent, setting up a corporate planning system will involve the introduction of planning *ab initio* into all the organisation's principal areas of activity; but where, as in many large organisations, some form of forward planning and co-ordination has always been essential, the development of 'corporate' planning is concerned with widening the scope of planning to make it more comprehensive and in particular to cover future financial prospects. (Such a development of corporate or strategic planning from physical planning, concerned mainly with how to meet future demand in terms of, say, tonnes of steel or megawatts of electrical generating capacity, is common to many capital intensive industries.)

The transition to corporate planning involves the introduction of four new elements:

1 financial evaluation;
2 consideration of alternatives;
3 broader coverage;
4 formulation of a long-term strategy.

Financial Evaluation

Financial evaluation involves examining the possible effect on future revenue, costs and profits of any course of action together with the capital expenditure required. The evaluation of investment proposals tends to be taken for granted, but the evaluation of strategies for parts or the whole of the business is less well established.

The feasibility of quantifying the possible effects on future profits of major policy decisions depends partly on the nature of the decision. For example, evaluation of a plan for rationalising production facilities may be very similar in nature to evaluation of a series of investment projects — feasible, but subject to all the customary errors and uncertainties of such exercises. On the other hand, evaluation of the net cost or benefit of a plan to establish single status for blue-collar and white-collar workers is well nigh impossible. The costs of upgrading the pension scheme and employment conditions for manual workers can be calculated, but no quantitative estimate can be made of the long-term advantages that it is hoped to achieve from such a change. The attempt to evaluate major decisions in financial terms is, however, an essential discipline, not solely in terms of the use of the results as an aid in decision-making, but also because it demands detailed consideration of the gains and losses likely to be involved. Indeed, resistance to such attempts frequently arises from the likelihood of the results being unpalatable rather than from the intrinsic difficulties of evaluation. We shall return to the problems of financial evaluation in the next chapter.

Consideration of Alternatives

The second contribution that the corporate planner can make to improving the decision-making process is to emphasise the need to consider the relevant alternatives. While this may at first sight seem an obvious thing to do, there are always strong pressures working the other way. The first and most justifiable is that managerial time is limited and the elaboration of alternatives may not be worth the effort involved. Very often, however, the reluctance to examine alternatives merely reflects the extent to which those making the proposals are wedded to their own particular solution, even if the possible alternatives have not been properly examined.

In the case of new plant proposals, for example, consideration of alternatives may involve considerable expenditure of time by engineering and accounting staff in preparing cost estimates for alternative plant configurations or locations. The variety of alternatives to be evaluated has thus to be judged in the light of the magnitude of the decision and the extent to which there is reasonable scope for argument about the choices involved. There are always, however, two essential alternatives to be considered: (a) the proposal under consideration ('the developed case') and (b) carrying on with the minimum essential change (the 'base case'). It is more practical to define the 'base case' in terms of minimum change rather than no change, because if, for example, the proposal is to build a new plant, the relevant alternative is to inject sufficient capital into the old plant to keep it going, rather than doing nothing at all so that production grinds to a halt. (There is always a temptation to justify massive expenditure on the grounds that if nothing is done the situation will become impossible!)

Broader Coverage

The 'corporate' aspect of corporate planning is essentially a matter of coverage — in principle the plan should cover all the activities of the organisation in question (e.g. works and products) and all the functional aspects of management (finance, production, sales, personnel, etc.). This does not rule out the preparation of 'corporate' plans for individual subsidiaries or operating divisions, as well as for the main company, but it means that they should in each case be comprehensive in terms of the organisation they purport to cover.

It would be misleading to imagine that corporate planning always lives up to this ideal; in particular, the emphasis may be heavily financial with only limited consideration of, say, manpower problems. The test is that its coverage should be sufficiently comprehensive to provide a reliable guide to action for that particular firm.

Formulation of Strategy

Finally, the development of long-term planning should be linked to the formulation of strategy in two ways. The more detailed work of planning should help to arrive at realistic and well-considered strategies, as well as providing an efficient means of implementing them. One of the most important facets of planning work is undertaking *ad hoc* 'planning studies', as opposed to the regular planning process. By 'planning studies' I mean the examination of particular strategic problems as a basis for strategic decisions — for example, the adoption of a new technology, or expansion into a new area. Such studies are often more fundamental to the future of the organisation than the regular planning exercises, as they set the direction for many years, and the merits of the decision can to a large extent determine the success or failure of the enterprise.

Hierarchy of Plans

Just as the nature of the key strategic problems facing management will vary from enterprise to enterprise, so will the content of their planning work and the methods by which it is undertaken. In the simplest terms, however, there are three essential layers in any formal planning system: strategy; long-term development plan; and short-term operating plan. The first two can be treated together and covered in one document although they are conceptually different, for example in detail and precision. They are both essentially about new initiatives and changing course. The short-term operating plan has to be considered separately in an organisation with long lead times for new projects, new products, etc. But in periods of crisis the operating plan may become the dominant vehicle for considering and executing major changes with long-term implications, such as plant closures or cuts in manning. One of the features militating against sound strategic decisions is that it is possible to manage without a long-term plan but not without an operating plan.

The structure of formal plans in a large organisation is sometimes referred to as the 'hierarchy' of plans and can be viewed as a pyramid with the corporate strategy and long-term plan at the top, and then the more detailed plans of different divisions and functions needed to implement them spread out below (see figure 8.1). The divisional plans are in turn based on plans for individual works and departments. In other words, the structure of plans naturally follows the organisational structure and hierarchy. In most cases there will be a similar hierarchical pattern for both long-term and short-term planning.

Bottom-up or Top-down?

A distinction is frequently made between 'bottom-up' and 'top-down' planning in the sense that the corporate plan may either be regarded as built up from a series of plans for the component parts or as handed down from above by the Chairman or Chief Executive. No effective plan can be based on either of these extremes, but must contain something of each. The data and forecasts needed to prepare a

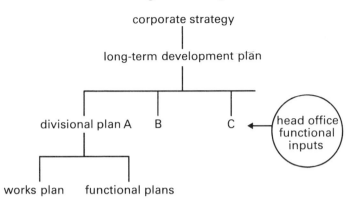

Figure 8.1   Hierarchy of plans

plan must be sought from many parts of the organisation and are not a prerogative of the centre. But the various parts of the organisation cannot be regarded merely as suppliers of data. They need to be involved more actively in the preparation of the plan. On the other hand, the final plan should not be just a collection of the individual aspirations of the constituent units. For one thing, their demand for investment funds would most probably exceed the total that could be made available. More fundamentally, such a plan would be unlikely to have any coherent strategic rationale. The responsibility of top management for determining the strategy of the organisation as a whole must be reflected in a major contribution from them in determining the thrust of the plan. Indeed, if the Chairman or Chief Executive is a person with creative flair and vision, this should inspire the whole planning exercise.

The problem is not whether the planning exercise should be bottom-up or top-down, but how to organise it in such a way as to combine as wide an element of participation as possible with top management control to ensure the requisite common purpose and strategy.

The question of participation is bound up with that of secrecy. There are certain elements in strategy formulation or planning which are difficult to discuss widely within the organisation. First, there are questions of commercial secrecy, of which the most delicate are merger or take-over plans. A high degree of confidentiality may also be necessary on plans to attack or out-manoeuvre a competitor, or for the development of new products or methods. Secrecy in these fields is mainly designed to prevent people outside the organisation knowing what is happening.

The second type of issue which leads to restrictions in the number of those involved arises when top management wishes to conceal something from the staff. The most frequent case here is that of closures or redundancies. These are the most difficult issues of all and the biggest obstacle to participation in planning. There are two stages involved here. The first is the exploration of alternatives. It is reasonable for a limited number of people in top management or the planning staff to examine hypothetical closures and manpower reductions. The problem is to decide at what stage management and employees concerned should become involved in the deliberations, in face of the difficulty of persuading any group of people to agree to the closure of their works or department if they will lose their jobs in the process. It is considerably easier to have widespread participation in planning as long as no redundancies (particularly compulsory redundancies) are involved. The Japanese policy of lifetime employment and the concept of widespread participation are thus closely linked. We return to this question in the final chapter.

Planning Cycles

While the determination of broad strategy or policy will tend to take place at irregular intervals, maybe of several years, formulation of detailed plans needs to follow a more regular, annual, pattern or cycle. This enables the planning exercise to make use of, and feed back into, the various shorter-term annual management exercises like the formulation of operating and capital budgets, sales forecasting, revision of standard costs, etc.

To set up the work needed to prepare a corporate plan, it is essential that an appropriate proposal should be put to the Chairman, Chief Executive and/or Board and that it should be properly understood and discussed by them. The amount of work involved and the sensitivity of the issues at stake are such that any attempt by the Planning Department or staff member responsible to try to set the exercise in motion solely on his or her own initiative is likely to prove disastrous. Such a proposal should first outline the nature of the exercise. It should then discuss its general purpose, namely, the main issues on which decisions are required. It should make clear the period of time to be covered. It should also clarify the areas of the business to be covered and the functional aspects: for example, are partly owned subsidiaries expected to participate; to what extent is the research and development side expected to make a contribution? Otherwise, those conducting the exercise may find themselves without the necessary authority to complete the work.

The proposal to the Board should also set out clearly the procedure to be followed and the dates for completion of the various stages. The key assumptions to be adopted need to be set out and agreed — for example, future inflation, exchange rates, any key political assumptions. The broad nature of the information and forecasts to be requested from divisions or functions must be outlined, and also what they are expected to do in the way of putting forward proposals for new projects of various kinds. Planning inevitably involves some danger of offending people's susceptibilities, because a plan (almost by definition) limits managers' freedom of action. It is therefore essential for the initiators both to pave the way by discussion with key personnel and to get clear backing from top management.

The timetable will then show the dates for getting in the various contributions, putting together alternatives, evaluating them, drawing up proposals, discussion by the Board (and/or its appropriate committee) and taking the final decisions. The whole exercise may take six months in a large organisation or even the best part of a year.

Investment Planning

Investment in new plant is one of the main instruments of strategic change, and a key element in most long-term plans. Conversely, major investment decisions must be taken in the context of long-term strategies and plans. Such decisions should be seen as part of a chain of events, starting from the formulation of strategy and ending with the full operation of the plant. This process might be summarised as follows:

1 Consider strategic alternatives
2 Settle strategy
3 Consider investment alternatives
4 Determine preferred investment
5 Prepare detailed investment proposal
6 Consider and approve project
7 Order and construct plant
8 Commission and run-in new plant

Students in either management or economics will find an extensive literature on the evaluation of investment projects and criteria for deciding whether or not to go ahead with a specific project. Comparatively little is said about the *formulation* of projects — that is, the process of drawing up the precise proposal under consideration. Yet it is the quality of the projects put forward, whether as a result of flair and inspiration, good design or thorough analysis of the problem, that determines the future success of the business. The Yes/No decision-making process, at the point where the Board makes the final decision to go ahead or not, can only stop uneconomic projects going forward; it cannot of itself produce creative and successful investments.

In so far as there can be any prescription for successful investment, it must cover the whole process of preparing such projects, and then implementing them, which precedes and follows the actual decision to go ahead. The initial impetus to a major project is likely to come from the broad strategy adopted or under consideration for the enterprise as a whole, or for a particular product group or sector of activity. In a capital-intensive industry such as chemicals, the strategy and the investment in capacity to achieve it may be inseparable. In other cases, for example the automobile industry, the decision to develop a new product may be more fundamental than the decision on the investment in the plant needed to produce it. In all cases, however, the two basic points are that the investment must be seen as part of the strategy adopted, and that a consideration of alternatives is an essential precondition for arriving at a successful final proposal.

Thus the *broad* proposal to build a new plant may emerge initially as part of the preferred strategy after consideration of various alternative strategies. The *precise* nature of the plant will then emerge later as the result of a continuous process of considering detailed alternatives during the process of formulation. Hence it is important that the process of preparing the project should be in the hands of a management team representing all the relevant functions, and not regarded as something to be left solely to the engineers. The preparation of the project should from the start be in the hands of a nominated project manager. He may be part-time in the case of a minor project, but with a major project this will be his full-time responsibility. Frequently the project manager is the person who will be responsible for the execution of the project or the ultimate running of the new plant. While the engineering function is central to the process of project preparation, because it physically defines the project, the project manager must co-ordinate staff work from a variety of functions. Both design and evaluation depend on the participation of the market forecasters; the accountants are involved in estimating capital and operating costs; technical advice is required from the research and development departments; the personnel function will advise on labour aspects; and there may well be transport and supplies aspects to be considered. Normally there would be a project committee working on the preparation of a major proposal. Its report would include sections dealing with the various functional aspects of the project, the plan for constructing it and the financial evaluation. This would be put to the Board or other appropriate authority for approval before contract negotiations were started.

The analysis of the factors affecting the profitability of the project (markets to be entered, prices, location of plant, capacity, etc.) while the project is still being formulated is likely to be more beneficial than the final evaluation when the project has been fully formulated. The process of evaluation should be regarded as a means of arriving at the best possible project, rather than merely a guide to determining whether a specific project should be approved or rejected. What is said later about detailed evaluation techniques should be seen in that context.

In making investment decisions, the two key financial questions are:

1 Is the investment likely to be profitable?
2 Will we be able to afford the cost of undertaking?

To answer the second question, it is necessary to examine the forecast cash out-flow for the project in question in relation to that of the firm as a whole. (This out-flow will arise not only during the period of construction, but also while working capital is being built up and then during the commissioning and working-up period before full output is reached.) This is one reason why large firms undertaking a number of investment projects need an investment programme (for, say, five years) as a basic feature of their planning. This enables them to keep total investment expenditure within limits set by the company's overall financial position and also provides a means of monitoring and controlling expenditure.

Investment Programmes

An investment programme in a large company will generally consist of provision for (a) individual projects over a certain size and (b) divisional budgets for small projects. This would reflect the general pattern under which schemes over £X have to be approved centrally, and schemes under £X can be approved by Divisions against an agreed budget for divisional schemes. (Within Divisions, a similar type of devolution will probably be in operation, with schemes between £Y and £X having to be approved at Divisional level while schemes under £Y can be approved at Works level.)

Since the typical large scheme takes three to four years to construct in this country, a five-year investment programme will consist of:

1 expenditure on projects already started;
2 expenditure on projects started early in the programme and finished within the period covered;
3 expenditure on some projects started but not finished in the period.

This is depicted graphically in figure 8.2.

The Board will probably settle the investment programme annually but it may need more frequent adjustment, particularly if there are cash-flow difficulties. The process of drawing up the programme will be to consider potential projects for inclusion against the finance available in the light of preliminary knowledge about the merits of each project. For many unapproved projects, knowledge of their probable profitability may well be sketchy because they are in the early stages of formulation; or, in the case of projects to be undertaken at the end of the programme period, because no start has yet been made to draw them up. Thus the programme is more tightly defined in the early years and more tentative in later years.

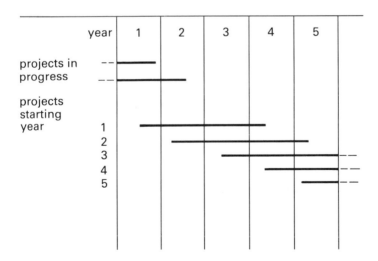

Figure 8.2   Five-year investment programme

Planning in the Large Integrated Firm

Long-term planning tends to be most highly developed in the large integrated firm: 'large' in the sense that it has to be split into identifiable management units (i.e. has some form of divisional structure) and 'integrated' in the sense that the operation of the parts is interconnected. In extreme cases this interconnection may be physical, as in the case of the electricity generating system or the telecommunications network; but more often the interaction springs from the fact that different production facilities can supply the same or overlapping markets (e.g. oil companies and airlines). Planning in such organisations is essential to ensure the necessary co-ordination of development, apart from any question of trying to formulate and implement the optimum strategy. This need may be greater in the case of long-term development plans and major investment decisions than current operations. For example, the Ford Motor Company may devolve responsibility for current sales and operations to Ford of Europe but retain central control over the location of investment in new plant and the introduction of new models, which have to be considered on a world-wide scale.

The way in which planning is conducted in such enterprises will depend partly on their formal organisation. There are basically two types of divisional organisation: area-based or product-based. In either case, the Managing Director of each Division has functional directors (finance, marketing, etc.) under his 'line' command. The relationship between the Divisional functional directors and their Head Office functional department (where there is one) is weaker than and subservient to their line relationship with their managing directors. This type of organisation tends to be the norm in large manufacturing firms.

The alternative form of organisation, less frequently seen in large organisations, is an extension of the small-firm structure wherein the basic split is into functional departments. In the large firm, these departments become Divisions, and a geographical or product breakdown is also introduced, cutting across the functional organisation. But, in contrast to the 'true' Divisional structure, the area director's or co-ordinator's authority over functional staff is weaker than the link to their functional departments. Such a form of organisation is inevitably much more centralised than the area or product Division type of organisation; it tends to be limited to situations where the physical production facilities are highly integrated, or to firms in service industries.

The approach to planning must reflect the formal organisation and the power structure within it. With a decentralised Divisional structure, the planning process must actively involve Divisional management and there should be a clearly recognisable Divisional component within the plan. In a similar way, the stronger the functional organisation, the stronger the functional breakdown of the plan. This reflects the fact that the organisational structure will (or should) be geared to the nature of the business and the power structure within it. Having said this, however, it should also be remembered that the organisational structure of the business will tend to be dictated by the day-to-day needs of its shorter-term operating characteristics rather than by considerations of long-term development. This is most clearly apparent in the holding company/subsidiary company organisation of the conglomerate. There must, almost inevitably, be a greater degree of centralisation in strategic planning than in operational management. This poses problems for those engaged in planning, which can only be resolved by a combination of top-level support and good relations with Divisional staff.

It also follows that long-term strategic issues frequently come up in a form that cuts across organisational boundaries and requires a special exercise by an *ad hoc* working group. The membership of such groups has both to represent the main functional and works interests involved, and to mobilise the expertise and personalities most likely to devise an effective solution. Setting up such groups with the right terms of reference and appropriate membership is one of the most important managerial tasks in this field and may require as much, or more, effort and skill than the study itself. Thus, I would add to Russell Ackoff's description of planning as a 'complex and difficult intellectual activity', that it is also a delicate, diplomatic one.

Multinationals

Large integrated multinationals (e.g. major oil companies and automobile producers) have to cope with the additional dimension of choice between countries when considering their development strategies. Such choice tends to raise very long-term issues where calculation has to give way to strategic judgement. Whereas exporters have to take strategic decisions on entry to foreign markets, multinational producers have to take strategic decisions on production in foreign countries to supply customers in that market or in neighbouring countries. In the case of manufacturing companies, the overriding factor may be a desire to get behind protective barriers hindering exports. These may be quantitative restrictions in the case of developing countries or tariff barriers as with the EEC. An alternative motive may be to exploit low production costs arising from cheap labour, or easy access to materials. In other cases, circumstances in the base country may drive further expansion abroad. For example, at one point in the 1970s the Japanese steel industry adopted a strategy of siting further expansion abroad because it was running out of suitable sites at home and pollution problems were becoming severe.

In considering production costs in different countries, the relative position is dominated by the level of exchange rates, which tend to vary over a much shorter time-scale than that relevant to strategic decisions about building new plant or acquiring production facilities. This means that decisions have to be taken on a broad economic and political assessment of the likely position over a period of years. Such an assessment will include political issues, such as the future stability of the country; the terms and conditions of any financial assistance from the government; the tax position; and the level of tariffs and import controls. Multinationals producing the same or similar products in a number of different countries may vary their production schedules at the margin according to current levels of costs; but having taken the strategic decision to produce in, say, the UK, they cannot suddenly reverse that decision if sterling strengthens in an unforeseen way.

Strategic planning in a large multinational can play a particularly important part in holding the company together. To do so it needs to be clearly organised on a regular and well-understood basis.

System Approach

When analysing planning problems in a large integrated company it is essential to adopt what might be termed a 'system approach'. The word 'system' is now used widely in a variety of contexts, but here it means simply that it is essential to examine the repercussions of decisions affecting any one part of the system (e.g. division or works) on the system or company as a whole. The need for such an approach is self-evident when the organisation is running a physical network such as a railway or gas distribution system; it is not always immediately obvious where it consists of a number of separate works as, for example, an airline or a steel company.

To take a major steel company as an example. It will typically consist of a number of different works each producing a group of products, with most products produced at more than one works. There may well be some transfers of semi-finished steel between works. The works will tend to draw their coking coal, iron ore and scrap from the same suppliers through a centrally organised supply operation. The same and different products from the various works will very often be sold in the same markets or even to the same major customer. Such an integrated production system is illustrated in figure 8.3. In these circumstances strategic decisions about any one works or product cannot be taken in isolation.

This is not difficult to grasp at corporate level, but for managers or trade unions at individual works things can look very different − particularly if they are encouraged from an operational point of view to look at themselves as a profit centre. An extreme example of such a conflict arises when it is argued that a works which is in profit, (i.e. the revenue from its sales exceeds its costs) should be closed down and its load transferred to another works which is at present underemployed. Such a transfer may reduce

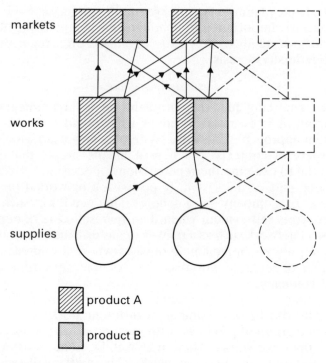

markets

works

supplies

product A

product B

Figure 8.3 Production system

system costs and improve the profitability of the organisation as a whole, but the individual works cannot be expected to take kindly to such a proposition. Such cases are not common, but it is not unusual in a recession for there to be a situation in which profitability could be improved by closing one works out of a number producing the same product, without there necessarily being a clear-cut case in terms of costs and efficiency, access to the market, etc., for closing one particular works rather than another.

When formulating a plan for the organisation as whole, it is natural to take a corporate view and consider the implications of the development of parts of the company on its overall profitability. But when undertaking planning studies to formulate strategies for particular products or activities, it is necessary to consider carefully how to ensure that all *significant* system effects are taken into account without extending the coverage of the exercise unduly. The object must be to define the 'system' to be considered so that it covers as small an area as possible without omitting any important ramifications. This applies to all aspects of such problems, from setting up the working groups which will undertake the study to defining the area to be covered if a computer model is to be constructed. The same principle applies to the evaluation of major investment projects (see chapter 9).

Computer Models

The use of computer models is a natural adjunct of the system approach. The essence of any model is that it is a simplified representation of reality, but embodies the significant factors adequately enough to give a satisfactory answer to the problem in hand. Simplification and adequacy are the two, potentially conflicting, requirements. For example, the firm may make hundreds of thousands of products of different dimensions or specifications, but it may be necessary and adequate to group them into a small number of categories when constructing a model of its production capacity and costs. Unnecessary complexity is a hindrance, not a help, in understanding and analysing the problem at issue. Nevertheless, even with considerable simplification the data to be handled remain complex, and it is only the advent of the computer that has made the use of models a practical proposition.

Models are particularly useful in handling planning problems in large integrated enterprises with a number of inter-related plants, especially for financial evaluation purposes.[4] A typical model will represent costs and capacity at the various works, and prices and sales volume in the markets they serve. The basic data on costs and capacity at existing plant will be derived from the standard cost system, where there is one; if not, from cost and technical data. The market data will come from market forecasts. Estimates of costs and capacity at possible new plant will be derived from work on investment proposals (see chapter 9). The model can then be used to estimate revenue, costs and profits year by year for different configurations of new and existing plant on various assumptions about market potential (see figure 8.4).

A technical feature of such a model is its ability to allocate a particular volume of sales and output between works (and to specify any inter-works transfers) in order to enable the cost of producing it to be calculated. It thus requires a set of 'allocation rules' to do this. These are frequently specified in terms of cost minimisation, thus enabling a linear programming model to be used. But sometimes the degree of simplification embodied in the models means that a linear programming model, even with appropriate constraints, may give unrealistic answers, and more specific allocation rules may give a more realistic answer.

Within a large organisation, planning models may be constructed at several different levels of the organisation, for example at corporate, divisional and works levels, or for different products or groups of products. The higher the organisational level and the greater the area of activity covered, the less is the amount of detail required on individual plant or products.

Somewhat similar models may be used for operational and development planning. But different end purposes usually lead to different requirements. A typical requirement for an operational model is to help determine the work load on individual works in a forthcoming period: scheduling tanker movements in oil companies or aircraft movement in an airline would be similar problems. Models designed to deal with these problems require enough detailed information on the product mix of the order load and the production capability of each works to come to a realistic detailed answer. Development planning models, on the other hand, are frequently concerned mainly with calculating the probable cost of satisfying a demand forecast, and the loading of individual works is only an incidental part of this process. Operational models are thus often too detailed in certain respects for longer-term planning purposes, and simpler

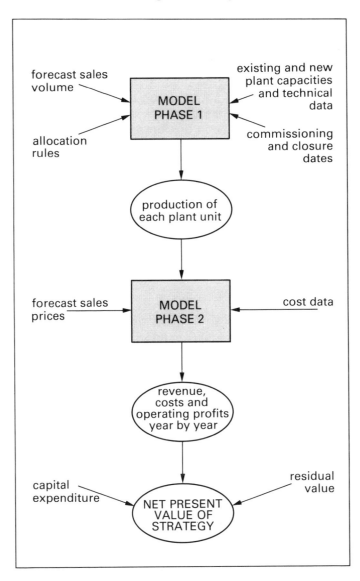

Figure 8.4 Evaluation model

models may be better adapted to the examination of varying plant configurations and market forecasts.

Apart from the skills required to construct the model itself, models of this type involve a great deal of effort and organisation to collect the data. It is not just a matter of collecting information about things as they are. Plans for the future have to be based on assessments of prices, sales and costs as they may be in the future. If new plant is under consideration, estimates of its capital and running costs are required. Where the data required involve a variety of works and functions, it can only be collected with the agreement and co-operation of management in these areas. Thus, the use of such models is only practical when their construction is part of a planning exercise involving those responsible for supplying the data in question. The proliferation of computers does little to facilitate the use of such models; the key factor is the availability of the necessary information or forecasts.

Advantages and Disadvantages of Models

There are both advantages and disadvantages in using computer models of this type. The main advantages are:

1 The discipline of model-building and data collection calls for rigorous thinking and clear definition of such concepts as, for example, effective capacity (see chapter 9).
2 The computer can handle a large volume of data. (It is important, however, to avoid the temptation to throw in unnecessary detail in an attempt to carry conviction.)
3 Speed of calculation. Once the model has been set up and the data are available, variations in proposals and assumptions can be speedily investigated.
4 The model should thus encourage the examination of alternative proposals and forecasts. The strength of the model-building approach should lie in its ability to answer the question, 'What if?'

On the other hand, the use of models also carries a number of disadvantages:

1 A high initial investment is required, both in skilled manpower to build the model and in providing the necessary data and forecasts. The collection of information for models tends to take more effort than its collection for *ad hoc* exercises because it is more difficult to skip problem areas which may not be of immediate relevance, and there has to be greater emphasis on uniformity and completeness.

2 The model becomes useless unless the data are regularly updated, and it may be difficult to get agreement to update it annually when it is not clear where, and for what purposes, the model may be used.

3 Decision-makers are allergic to the 'Black-Box' effect, when numbers are thrown into the computer and only the model-builders understand the principles on which the calculations are based. It is essential that the rules of the game should be understood and agreed on by everyone involved.

4 The use of models may create organisational tensions which hinder the objective analysis of the strategic problems under consideration.

The last point is part of the reason why the use of planning models has remained less popular than might be expected with the rapid spread of computers and computerised information in recent years. There are serious managerial problems in constructing models which span different divisions and functions in a large organisation. Those involved frequently raise considerable doubts about the time needed to supply the data and the efficacy of the model. But behind these overt objections lies the fear of loss of power or influence if data is supplied freely to feed into a model under someone else's control at head office. Often such a model will centralise calculations which were formerly spread over different parts of the organisation and thus ensured the participation in the exercise of the managers concerned. The fear is that the use of the model will relegate those involved to mere providers of data whilst others come up with recommendations that may be unpalatable to their works or function. This fear can only be overcome by making any such model clearly the servant and not the master of those involved in, and affected by, any planning exercises of this nature.

Such difficulties do not exist when the information is already available to those concerned, and the relative popularity of desk-top financial planning models probably reflects this.[5]

Similar factors go some way to explain the fact that the use of computerised networks are much further advanced for operational and accounting purposes than for the provision of statistical and financial information as an aid to management decisions. The other major reason is the effort required to organise the mass of operational data into an intelligible form for this purpose.

Notes

1 Russell L. Ackoff, *A Concept of Corporate Planning*, 1970.
2 Sir Basil Henry Liddell Hart, *Strategy: The Indirect Approach* (4th edn), 1967.
3 For an account of planning at NASA see James M. Beggs, 'Leadership – The NASA Approach', *Long Range Planning*, April 1984.
4 For a review of the use of planning models in nationalised industries see Ann P. Brown, 'Planning Models', in John Grieve Smith (ed.), *Strategic Planning in Nationalised Industries*, 1984.
5 For an assessment of the spread of model-building in UK companies see Peter H. Grinyer and Jeff Wooller, *Corporate Models Today* (2nd edn), 1978.

9

Financial Evaluation

Evaluation and Forecasting

Any quantitative analysis of alternative strategies and plans (whether in physical or financial terms) depends on the use of forecasts, since it is concerned with trying to assess the future consequences of current decisions. Such analysis is thus necessarily subject to various degrees of uncertainty. Some elements in the calculation may seem relatively firm, either because they are based on past experience or because they represent a continuation of current conditions; but it is essential to remember that the assumption of a maintenance of the status quo or the continuation of past trends is just as much a forecast as any other assumption about the future, and similarly subject to error.

Even the simplest type of investment decision − to replace an old machine without any consequent change in output, for example − involves forecasting. The cost of the machine bought off the shelf may be known if the decision is an immediate one, but the estimated savings in running costs and maintenance are a forecast. The physical savings may be a good forecast based on past experience, but the translation of these into money terms depends on forecasting future wages and material costs. The degree of conjecture involved increases with the extent to which the new project represents a departure from present conditions. In the case of investment in plant, which involves an increase in output, it is necessary to forecast the increase in the volume of sales, which may depend partly on demand and partly on the effective increase in capacity; it is also necessary to forecast selling prices and running costs.

Financial evaluation is a particular form of forecasting − one that is an essential element in analysing alternative strategies and plans and arriving at strategic decisions. There are two types of financial forecast. The first is an estimate of the profitability of the enterprise (or part of the enterprise) in *absolute* terms on certain assumptions about the firm's own policy and likely developments in the world around it; for example, a particular strategic alternative. The second is an estimate of the effect of a particular management decision (for example, to undertake a major investment) and is an estimate of the *difference* in profitability likely to result from the decision: this involves forecasting what will happen (a) if the action is taken and (b) if it is not (the so-called 'developed' and 'base' cases). These two approaches may be defined as estimating 'absolute' and 'differential' profitability, respectively. Both involve forecasting the same variables: in particular, revenue, costs, profits and capital expenditure.

Financial evaluations of particular strategies or plans tend to be estimates of 'absolute' profitability, which may then be compared to establish the relative profitability of different alternatives. Investment evaluations (or the evaluation of particular strategic decisions), on the other hand, are essentially a matter of forecasting the difference in profitability resulting from the decision in question, and hence are based on the 'differential' approach.

Financial forecasts for a firm, or one of its divisions or subsidiaries, may be derived in varying degrees of detail. It is, however, essential: (a) to start from a basis of actual figures for the most recent period available; (b) to consider past trends; (c) to identify the main factors which are likely to lead to changes in future; and (d) to consider the possible effects of variations in the assumptions arising from the most significant uncertainties. There is no standard method for projecting any of the variables involved; each firm tends to evolve its own methods.

Internal Forecasts

Financial forecasts depend both on forecasting external or environmental factors, such as the demand for the firm's products or the price of materials, and also factors internal to the firm, such as labour productivity or materials usage. We discussed in chapter 3 the problems of assessing the impact of environmental change on a firm, and forecasting variables subject mainly to external influences. There are, however, equally difficult problems (though different in nature) in forecasting internal factors; though these are subject to influence by management, they are not for the most part subject to *absolute* management control − if they were, industrial efficiency would be very much higher than it actually is.

The treatment of such factors raises difficult issues, best described in terms of the distinction between (a) management targets or objectives (e.g. to cut down yield losses by 10 per cent) and (b) the most realistic or central forecast as to what will actually happen. This dilemma arises in all the main determinants of efficiency affecting future operating costs. It also arises, for example, in the speed and cost of completion of capital projects. The completion dates set for projects tend to be targets and projects are more frequently finished late than early. It is not always easy to build in a realistic allowance for unforeseen delays because of the feeling that any acknowledgement of the possibility of delay is more likely to make it happen. The same considerations apply to any allowance for failure to reach targets for reducing manning or improving yields. Yet wherever management does not have the absolute power to control results (i.e. in almost every field of activity), the assumptions about the future involve a major element of forecasting. It is therefore essential for those involved in forecasting for planning purposes to be able to handle such delicate subjects in terms of realistic forecasts as opposed to management targets. Very often the simplest way to do this is by inserting a 'contingency allowance' to allow for failure to reach the target. Unless this problem is tackled carefully, the plan will tend to have a built-in element of over-optimism, particularly when the external environment is hostile. The reverse can, of course, also apply − that is, excessive management caution in setting targets in order to be sure of over-achieving them; but this is less likely when there is strong central management vetting the objectives.

Key examples of the internal factors, forecasts of which are important, range from investment to sales. The eventual costs and completion dates of *major projects* taking several years to complete always involve an element of forecasting. When *new products* are under consideration, the cost of development, date of introduction, detailed product characteristics and actual manufacturing cost have a large element of uncertainty, and realistic forecasting in this field is always extremely difficult. In the case of *operating costs*, technical standards, including labour and material inputs and finished product yields, are never rigidly determined, but the improvements obtainable over a period of years are uncertain. In capital-intensive industries, the *effective capacity of the plant* is also uncertain, because of variations both in availability and in maximum output when in operation. Finally, in so far as sales depend on the firm's own marketing efforts, the effectiveness of any specific measures to increase sales is nearly always highly speculative.

Thus the problems of forecasting cover not only the external factors usually considered in this context, but also the results of the firm's own attempts to manage the resources at its disposal.

Investment Evaluation

Investment evaluation is a fundamental aspect of financial evaluation for strategic purposes, both because investment in various forms is generally the key to implementing new strategies, and because the techniques of investment evaluation are also applicable to the evaluation of strategies involving a series of related capital expenditures.

To evaluate an investment project, forecasts are required of:

1 sales revenue;
2 operating costs (including commissioning and running in);
3 changes in working capital; and
4 fixed capital expenditure,

for both the base and the developed cases.

To estimate both revenue and operating costs it is necessary first to forecast the physical volume of sales and production. Initially, output will probably be limited by the rate at which production can be built up while the plant is working up. Later it may be limited either by demand or capacity.

Capacity and Plant Utilisation

Plant designers tend to work in terms of theoretical capacity of plant, in the sense of the maximum output obtainable per hour when it is operating normally. It is then necessary to discount theoretical capacity to arrive at the *effective* annual capacity, taking into account the maximum practical availability after allowing for down-time for maintenance, unscheduled breakdowns, etc.

It is, however, generally over-optimistic to assume 100 per cent utilisation of effective capacity even in times of high demand. For many products demand is subject to seasonal variations; hence it is not possible to work at the same rate throughout the year and respond promptly to customers' demands. The greater the amplitude of such variations, the lower the average level of utilisation. Taking a longer view, there is also the problem of fluctuations in demand from year to year, which tend to reduce the average level of plant utilisation over a period of years. Thus even if demand is expected to be broadly adequate to absorb the output of the plant, it is over-sanguine to assume that it will achieve 100 per cent utilisation of effective capacity over its working life, and it is necessary to arrive at a realistic figure for maximum practical utilisation.

Utilisation may, of course, be lower if demand is inadequate and the market share obtainable is insufficient to achieve maximum practical utilisation. The volume of sales and output from year to year in the evaluation exercise will then be determined primarily by demand rather than by capacity.

Price/Cost Ratio

Having forecast the volume of sales and output, it is necessary to forecast selling prices and production costs to arrive at revenue and costs, respectively. Forecasting prices is probably the most difficult and insecure part of the whole evaluation. There is no escape from the problem by assuming that prices will remain unchanged or go up in line with prices in general; that is just as significant a forecast as assuming an upward or downward change.

As with many other variables, it is important when considering the possible future behaviour of prices to distinguish between short-term cyclical movements and longer-term trends. Cyclical movements tend to be dominated by changes in market conditions. These may result from the impact of a business cycle affecting the general level of activity in the economy as a whole, or from special factors affecting that particular industry − for example, stock movements, a sudden increase or decrease in demand, a new entrant to the industry cutting prices, etc. Such movements need to be understood and analysed in forming a judgement as to how far present prices can be regarded as 'normal' or as cyclically low or high, and hence liable to be corrected either way. Longer-term trends are often more difficult to detect and hence in danger of being ignored.

There are two main influences on the long-term price/cost ratio. The first is from trends in demand/supply relationships. If capacity is liable to grow more rapidly than demand, then there is likely to be an adverse shift in price/cost relationships and vice versa. Such disparities may arise from a sudden burst of competitive investment conceived in a boom and coming to fruition a few years later. In products subject to international competition it may come more gradually, but more persistently, from the growth of new low-cost capacity in parts of the Third World.

The second and most inescapable adverse influence on the price/cost ratio is technical progress. One firm may build a plant today with a certain relationship prevailing between prices and input costs. In a few years' time another firm will build another, more efficient, plant and will be able to make a profit with a lower level of selling prices in relation to input prices. So selling prices tend to come down relative to input prices. Growing efficiency in operating the same plant will have the same effect. (In the country as a whole, where the majority of costs are represented by wages and salaries, this process shows up in the long-term trend for prices to rise more slowly than wages and salaries as productivity increases.)

Thus the normal long-term trend in most industries is for selling, or output, prices to rise more slowly than input prices as efficiency increases (see figure 9.1). This means that the operating profit on an investment tends to be greater in its early years than its later years, and it is important to recognise this fact in evaluating investments. This is, of course, well recognised where technical progress is rapid and plant needs to be written off quickly before it becomes technically obsolescent; but it is less well recognised in other industries where technical progress is slower but still significant.

In manufacturing industry, operating costs depend on (a) technical standards and (b) input prices. By 'technical standards' we mean the physical inputs of materials, energy, labour, etc., required per unit of output. When new plant is similar to that already in operation, the determination of technical standards is not too difficult. But with any new technology, the level of such standards in practice can only be forecast with a fair margin of error.

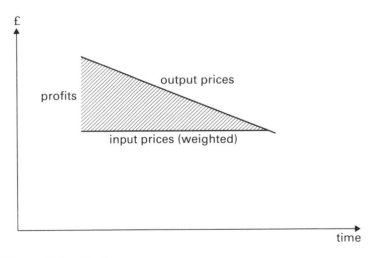

Figure 9.1   Profit squeeze

Forecasting input prices, including wages and salaries, raises problems similar in many ways to that of forecasting selling prices. Again, both the general effects of inflation and real changes need to be taken into account. In practice, it is generally only possible to forecast real changes for a limited number of items of particular importance for the process in question; but in virtually all cases this means allowing for the tendency for wages and salaries to increase in real terms in the long run.

For both forecast revenue and operating costs, the key year is the first year of full working (even though in principle the evaluation will be based on a forecast of profits over the whole life of the plant). It is often sufficient to estimate revenue and costs in detail for this year and then to derive forecasts for subsequent years by applying changes in sales and input prices, together with allowances for the effects of any changes in volume.

Investment Requirements

A new investment will involve a build-up of *working capital*, both in physical stocks and work-in-progress and in financial debtors and creditors. Changes in working capital each year must be estimated, both in order to determine the cash-flow position and to estimate the return on the project.

Finally, the eventual cost of the *fixed investment* itself must be estimated. Although this should be reasonably well determined at the time when the decision to go ahead is made, there will still be a number of elements of uncertainty in a large project. Even where fixed price contracts are in force, there may still be scope for design changes with consequent cost adjustments. Where there are provisions for escalation for rising prices and wages, the uncertainty about future inflation rates creates uncertainty about the eventual cost of the project in money terms, and any delay in completion will raise the final cost as well as affecting the timing of profits. In practice, major contracts tend to involve a grey area which has to be settled by negotiations before the final cost is determined. For these reasons, it is essential to embody an appropriate contingency allowance in the estimate of capital cost taken for evaluation purposes.

Differential Approach

In order to establish the effect of a project on the profitability of the company, it is necessary to make a forecast of future profits (a) without the project (the 'base case') and (b) with the project (the 'developed case'). The differences are then attributable to the project. Only when the project stands on its own as a separate enterprise is it sufficient to look solely at the profits in the 'developed case' because revenue, costs and profits in the 'base case' are all zero.

It can be quite misleading to try to establish the effects of an investment by comparing the estimated profitability of the company in a few years' time, after having made the investment, with profitability today. Such an approach ignores the question as to what would have happened to profits if the investment had not been made. If profits would have improved anyhow, such an approach overstates the benefits of the investment; on the other hand, if profits would otherwise have deteriorated, the benefits of the investment would be understated.

Thus it is essential to adopt the differential or 'incremental' approach in order to establish the increase in profits arising from the new investment *per se*. In adopting this approach, however, it is necessary to distinguish between investments which are reducing forecast losses and those which are increasing forecast profits. An investment in the first category may show a high incremental return but the activity concerned may still be running at a loss. Clearly in such cases the question of closing down that part of the business should be considered, and major investment should only be undertaken in exceptional circumstances. In evaluating such investments, allowance should be made for the fact that their life may be cut short by future closures.

In the intermediate case, where the forecast is for a loss without the investment and a profit if the investment is made, the profitability in the latter case needs to be compared with the alternative of closure or disposal: this may not be the same as zero profit because of (a) closure costs, which may be heavy, or (b) any proceeds from disposal of the assets.

Hence, in dealing with loss-making activities, it is necessary to compare: (a) the future profitability of the system if investment does take place and (b) the best alternative out of either continuing without the investment or shutting down the activity in question.

The other point at which ambiguity can arise is in the definition of the 'base case'. If, for example, an old plant will grind to a halt without a continuing injection of small capital expenditures, these should be taken into account in the base case rather than adopting a forecast of nil expenditure and hence complete disaster. In this sense the consideration of the profitability of additional investment in a continuing operation is always relative to some other hypothetical situation; and if some capital has to be spent in any event, the evaluation process is always a matter of comparing alternatives. This is another aspect of the point that the creative aspect of these analytical techniques is to assist managers to develop the best possible investment project, as opposed to the more negative one of helping to decide whether it should go ahead or not.

Evaluation Techniques

The object of investment evaluation is to compare the increase in profits expected from the project with the investment expenditure involved. The same principles apply to the evaluation of a strategy involving a series of investments in new plant, new models or market development. If the additional profit were to be the same in each year of the project's life, the measurement of the return would be simple, using the so-called *conventional* return, which equals the increase in profits divided by the capital cost. But such a measure takes no account of the time lag between capital expenditure and any increase in profits, or of year-to-year variations in profits.

Discounted Cash Flow (DCF) analysis takes into account differences in timing between outgoings and receipts, and variations from year to year. It does this by using a rate of interest to evaluate the benefit or cost of a payment in one year as opposed to another. Thus, with a 10 per cent rate of interest, £100 today will be worth £110 in a year's time, and conversely the discounted or 'present value' of £110 in a year's time is £100 today.

To establish the net benefit or cost of all the forecast outgoings and receipts associated with a project, DCF analysis involves discounting them all back to their *net present value* at a base date.

In algebraic terms, let

S_t = revenue in year t
C_t = current costs in year t
E_t = capital expenditure in year t
r = rate of interest

Then

$$\text{NPV} = \sum_{t=0}^{t=n} \frac{S_t - C_t - E_t}{(1 + r)^t}$$

where n is the life of the project (and any scrap value or residual debits or credits are included in the revenue or costs for the final year). If the resulting NPV is positive, then the receipts are worth more than the outgoings at the assumed rate of interest; if the NPV is negative, the discounted value of the outgoings is higher than that of the receipts.

An example of such a calculation is given in table 9.1. The net present value of an investment is the difference between the NPV of the 'developed case' (with the investment) and the NPV of the 'base case' (without the investment). In table 9.1 the NPV of the investment would be 32 *less* the NPV without it.

The *internal rate of return*, or *DCF return*, on a project is the rate of interest that gives a zero NPV for the project: that is, the rate of return at which the discounted profits attributable to the investment equal the discounted cost of the investment.

Evaluation: Real and Money Terms

In times of inflation it is necessary to distinguish between

TABLE 9.1 DCF Evaluation

Year	1	2	3	4	5
Revenue	—	50	100	110	120
Operating costs	—	40	60	66	73
Change in working capital	—	15	10	2	2
Fixed capital expenditure	30	20	—	—	—
Net cash flow	−30	−25	+30	+42	+45
(÷ discount factor)	(1.1)	(1.21)	(1.33)	(1.46)	(1.61)
Discounted cash flow (DCF)	−27	−21	+23	+29	+28
Net present value (NPV) at 10% +32 (5 years)					

TABLE 9.2 Money and Real Prices and Profits

Year	1	2	3	4
1. *Prices*				
(a) Money prices				
Selling prices	100	110	125	130
Input prices	100	112	128	135
(b) General price level	100	110	119	125
(*Inflation*)		(*10%*)	(*8%*)	(*5%*)
(c) Real prices*				
Selling prices	100	100	105	104
Input prices	100	102	108	108
2. *Profits*				
(a) Money profits	25	50	75	100
(b) General price level	100	110	119	125
(c) Real profits*	25	45	63	80

* At year 1 price levels.

making such evaluations in *real* or *money* terms. By the latter we mean the actual money values expected from revenue, costs and profits; by 'real' terms we mean the money values corrected for inflation: that is, divided or 'deflated' by an appropriate price index for the average rise in prices since the base date.

In table 9.2, with 10 per cent inflation a real rate of return of 2 per cent is equivalent to a money rate of return of 12.2 per cent (i.e., 1.10×1.02) — because if you invest £100, you need £112.20 at the end of a year to cover inflation of 10 per cent and give you a 2 per cent real rate of return. If you discount a set of forecasts in money terms with a 12.2 per cent discount rate, you will get the same result as discounting the same set of forecasts expressed in real terms with a 2 per cent discount rate. (Try it and see!)

In algebraic terms, let

r = money rate of interest
r' = real rate of interest
p = rate of inflation

Then

$$1 + r' = \frac{1 + r}{1 + p}$$

(and $r' \simeq r - p$)

Let S_t = revenue in year t in money terms, and S'_t = revenue in year t in real terms at year 0 prices, etc. Similarly, C and C' and E and E' represent current costs and capital expenditure in money and real terms, respectively. Then

$$S'_t = \frac{S_t}{(1 + p)} \text{ etc.}$$

$$\text{NPV} = \sum \frac{S' - C' - E'}{(1 + r')^t}$$

$$= \sum \frac{S - C - E}{(1 + r')^t (1 + p)^t}$$

$$= \sum \frac{S - C - E}{(1 + r)^t}$$

There are two alternative methods of evaluation:

1 express all the figures in money terms (i.e., the prices, profits, etc., you actually expect to get) and discount using the money rate of interest (e.g., the actual cost of borrowing);

2 express all the figures in real terms (i.e., with money prices, etc., deflated by the price index) and discount with the real rate of interest (i.e., the money rate less the rate of inflation).

If inflation is assumed to carry on at the same rate each year, both of the above approaches are equally serviceable. But if the inflation rate is expected to vary from year to year, the situation is more complicated. A steady real rate of interest will then imply a variable money rate or vice versa:

Example	*Year 1*	*Year 2*
Inflation rate	+ 10%	+ 5%
Real interest rate (constant)	+ 2%	+ 2%
Money interest rate (variable)	+ 12%	+ 7%
or Money interest rate (constant)	+ 12%	+ 12%
Real interest rate (variable)	+ 2%	+ 7%

Real or Money Approach?

There is, then, a choice as to whether to undertake a DCF calculation in money or in real terms. Money figures have the advantage of according with what you actually expect to happen, and to see in the accounts. People also often find it easier to make short-term forecasts (e.g., next year's wage levels or fuel prices) in money rather than real terms. If you are borrowing at a fixed rate of interest (in money terms), the money approach is the most relevant. On the other hand, if the forecasts are made in *real* terms the figures are at more familiar levels and much easier to 'get the feel of'. Attention is focused on real changes in prices (i.e., relative changes), which are generally the most fundamental.

The essential point is not that one approach is necessarily better than the other, but that the two alternatives tell the same story from a different angle.

Sensitivity Analysis

The previous discussion was concerned with the DCF approach to evaluating an investment, given the necessary year-by-year forecasts of revenue, costs, etc. over its life. Uncertainty about the future, however, is such that this evaluation may tell us about the profitability of the project on what is believed to be the most likely outcome, but tell us nothing about the likely profitability, if any, if the forecasts turn out to be wrong − as they almost certainly will. No evaluation is complete which does not consider the extent to which profitability could be affected by variations in the key forecasts; i.e. an analysis of its *sensitivity* to changes in the assumptions.

It is, for example, essential to consider variations in the forecasts of sales volume and prices and in the forecast relationship of selling prices to costs − generally the two key determinants of profitability. For major projects, variations in the cost and completion time of the investment itself should also be considered; so should variations in technical operating standards. A fairly typical sensitivity analysis might consider the effects on the NPV or DCF rate of return of the following magnitudes:

Sales volume	± 10%
Selling price	± 5%
Capital cost	+ 10%
Completion time	+ 30%
Operating standards	− 10%/+ 5%

It will be noted that the variations considered are not necessarily symmetrical with regard to the central forecast, since in certain cases (e.g. capital costs and construction time) adverse variations are more likely than favourable ones.

The procedure for sensitivity analysis is to vary each of these key assumptions in turn and calculate the effect on NPV or the rate of return. (It would be misleading to combine all the favourable or all the unfavourable assumptions in one calculation, as the probability of their all occurring together will be much lower than that of one of their variations occurring in isolation.) Examination of the effect on profitability of each of such variations spotlights the main areas where the project is likely to lose or gain from variations in the forecasts. When conducted at a formative stage in the process of formulating the project, such an analysis will help to arrive at a proposal which is as robust as possible in the face of these uncertainties. At the final decision-making phase it will help the Board to pay particular attention to the minimum conditions that need to be satisfied if the scheme is to have a reasonable chance of success.

Risk Analysis

A theoretically satisfactory way of assessing the effects of uncertainty (now made arithmetically acceptable by the advent of the computer) is the approach termed *risk analysis*. This involves expressing the possible magnitude of each variable in terms of a probability distribution, either in the form of a complete distribution curve or a series of ranges or numbers with probabilities attached to each. For example, the sales forecast might be expressed in terms of probabilities of the sales figure lying in each of four bands; the same with other key variables. It is then possible to calculate a probability distribution for the end-variable (e.g. profits) by permutating the various combinations. This will show both the most probable range for profits and also the probability of profits falling within higher or lower bands.

While, however, this approach is conceptually satisfying, it is not easy to apply in practice, because of the difficulty of assigning probabilities to different outcomes for the variables involved.[1] While it is often reasonable to say that sales could be 10 to 15 per cent lower than the central forecast, there is generally very little basis on which to express such an opinion in probabilistic terms. The approach is particularly difficult when a number of people are involved in the process with differing views about the probability of different results. Moreover, the results tend to concentrate attention on a probability distribution for the rate of return or NPV of the project, rather than an understanding of the key determinants of profitability. For these reasons formal risk analysis is used much less frequently than normal sensitivity analysis.

Comparing Projects

To compare the profitability of different investment projects, the first step is to compare the NPVs at one or more discount rates. This in effect compares the profit that each project would make after paying the specified rate of interest. Where the timing of the profits varies appreciably between the two projects, this method can be regarded as a comparison of the relative benefits of two profiles of capital expenditure and expected profits at a given discount rate. In some circumstances the relative merits of two schemes may be reversed by taking a higher or lower discount rate; for example, a high capital cost project, taking a long time to produce its full return, may have a higher NPV than a less capital-intensive solution when the comparison is made at a 5 per cent discount rate, but a lower NPV at a 10 per cent discount rate.

It should be noted that it is dangerous to compare projects solely by looking at their internal rate of return. Small remedial projects nearly always tend to show a higher return than major new projects, but this obscures the fact that the absolute addition to the company's profits may be much greater with the major project. On the other hand, from the point of view of risk, a project with a forecast NPV of £0.9 million and a return of 15 per cent is probably a better bet than one with an NPV of £1 million and a return of 10 per cent particularly if the minimum return acceptable is 10 per cent.

While discounted cash-flow analysis is the only satisfactory way of comparing projects where the cash flows show differing profiles over time, there are quite often alternatives where timing differences are not significant. A good example is the choice of location. Here a similar project in two alternative locations will probably show very similar *patterns* of profit over the years: the difference will be in the *level* of profits. In comparing projects in these circumstances the need is to investigate differences in costs (or revenue) in detail in a typical year, since such differences (e.g. in transport costs) are likely to persist throughout the period. Comparisons between the two projects can then be made on what might be called a 'snapshot' basis, by comparing the conventional return on capital (profits divided by capital expenditure) in a typical year.

Types of Option

In comparing alternative investments a type of option frequently encountered is the choice between modernising existing plant and investing in new plant. This is a situation where it is particularly important to examine the two different alternatives over a sufficient period of time. A typical pattern of cash flow in such cases is shown in figure 9.2.

Modernisation of existing plant typically involves relatively low capital injection now, but continued periodic injections of capital to keep the plant going. Production and quality problems are likely to persist and sooner or

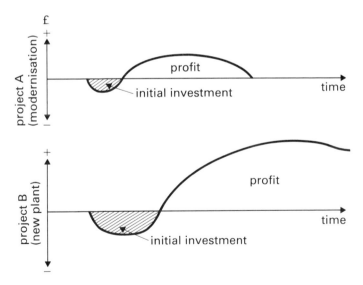

Figure 9.2 Cash flow with different types of investment option

later major new investment will be required. On the other hand, the new plant option will involve relatively high capital expenditure now, but there should on balance be less capital injection required than in the older plant (though new plant sometimes requires substantial capital injection in its early years to remedy design faults, etc.). With new plant, running costs should be lower and production more reliable, once the initial teething problems are overcome. Product quality should be improved. Very often the new plant can only be installed whilst at the same time increasing capacity, so that additional sales will be required.

One key factor in the choice is the speed of technical change (past and present): how out-of-date is the existing plant; how quickly will today's model be replaced by something better? The optimum moment for replacement from the point of view of technical progress is always difficult to determine: ideally it is when a substantial advance is about to be consolidated. Such a moment is much easier to identify after the event than at the time.

The cash outlook will also be an important determinant. A poor cash flow will tend to inhibit major investment, and to create a bias towards piecemeal modernisation.

Evaluation of Strategic Options

These methods of evaluating and comparing investment projects can also be applied to *strategic options*, that is different courses of action which may involve more than one investment scheme. An example would be the construction of (a) one major production plant together with a number of distribution depots and (b) a number of smaller production plants with distribution facilities attached. The DCF evaluation process is exactly the same, except that there will be a *series* of investments on the cost side.

Comparison of different strategies can raise in a more acute form the problem discussed above of comparing a major new investment with more modest expenditure on existing plant. The first alternative may involve no further major investment for fifteen years, but the second may envisage a major replacement in, say, ten years. How do you compare the two, given the difficulties of projecting revenue and costs ahead indefinitely?

It is necessary at this point to introduce the concept of *residual value*, that is, the value of an investment after a certain number of years' operation. For example, in the case of the major investment, it will have a substantial residual value after ten years, but the minor investment will have no residual value if the existing plant may have to be shut down by then. The residual value is in principle the net present value at the date in question (say, ten years hence) of the prospective profits from the asset over the remainder of its life. Using the same symbols as on p. 155, the residual value in year m is

$$\sum_{t = m}^{t = \infty} \frac{S_t - C_t - E_t}{(1 + r)^{t-m}}$$

where C_t may consist of injections of minor capital to keep the plant going. If this were to be calculated in the same amount of detail, however, as profits are being estimated for the first ten years, there would be no practical distinction between calculating a residual value and continuing the DCF calculation for an additional ten to fifteen years. The advantage of cutting short the number of years covered by the DCF evaluation in this way depends on finding a simple way of estimating residual value. The simplest of all is to say that the residual value is proportional to the estimated life of the plant, e.g. half the original cost when the plant is halfway through its life. This, however, generally tends to overstate the residual value, as profits tend to be higher (in real terms) in the earlier than in the later years. To get over this, an alternative approach is to assume that profits decline steadily from the point in question (e.g. year 10) to the estimated end of the plant's economic life (e.g. year 20). It is then very simple to calculate the residual value in year 10, giving an estimate of profits in that year.

The merit of the residual value concept lies not so much in the precise estimate (which is necessarily highly uncertain), but in providing a logical frame of analysis for considering the merits of different options which leave the enterprise in a substantially different position at the end of, say, ten years.

Corporate Finance

Investment evaluation techniques are designed to establish whether the return on the investment is likely to be adequate. There remains the question of whether the firm is in a position to finance the various investments which it has in mind. To answer the second question, the individual investments in a strategic plan need to be aggregated into an investment programme (see chapter 8, pp. 132–3); the total cost of that programme must then be considered in relation to a forecast of cash flow for the organisation as a whole, together with its ability and willingness to borrow or raise fresh capital if necessary. Thus the forecasts of (a) revenue, costs and profits and (b) capital expenditure for a particular strategy serve two purposes. The first is to establish whether the resulting profit is satisfactory; the second is to investigate whether the necessary investment can be financed.

The forecasts of overall corporate profits must therefore cover not only the end-point of the strategy but also the intermediate years, or path to that end-point. In addition to the need to examine the forecasts for intermediate years from a cash-flow/financing aspect, it is also necessary to consider whether the strategy involves any short-term effects on profits which may make it financially impractical or undesirable: for example, large-scale investments may have disruptive effects on production with a short-term loss of business and loss of profits at a time when investment in equipment and working capital is going to drain the cash flow. A further important aspect to be considered is the implications for dividend policy.

The examination of cash-flow and financing problems involves the extension of the profit and loss forecast into the capital account to build up a year-by-year picture of the cash position and flow of funds for investment. If new borrowing or fresh capital is required, the effect on the debt/equity ratio must be considered. Thus, for a strategy to be financially acceptable, it must both pass the test of showing an adequate level of profitability and involve a satisfactory picture as regards dividend distribution, the creation and use of reserves, and changes in borrowing and equity.

Note

1 For an example of its use in practice, see Robert F. Eggar and Michael M. Menke, 'An Inside View: Analysing Investment Strategies', *Planning Review*, May 1981, (reprinted in Milton Leontiades, ed., *Policy Strategy and Implementation*: *Reading and Cases*, 1983).

10

State Enterprises and Public Utilities

In previous chapters, most of the discussion has taken the problems of companies in the private sector as the norm. This reflects partly the fact that such companies are more numerous than their public sector counterparts, and partly the dominating influence on the subject of business schools and consultants in the United States where public enterprise is virtually non-existent. But no discussion of strategy formulation would be complete without consideration of the special problems of state-owned enterprises. Although the area of state ownership in the UK has been considerably reduced in the second half of the 1980s, state ownership still accounts for a significant proportion of industry in many parts of the world. Moreover, developments in Eastern Europe, Russia and China may, during the 1990s, create a major area of the world in which state enterprises operate in market, or part-market economies under varying degrees of political democracy.

In any state enterprise, its strategic problems are partly a reflection of the industry in which it is operating and partly its ownership *per se*. In countries with relatively small public sectors, state enterprises tend to be concentrated in special areas like public utilities such as water or telecommunications where social factors are particularly important, and state ownership is intended to ensure a distinctive style of management. In countries with relatively large public sectors, however, there will tend to be state enterprises operating in a variety of manufacturing industries: formulating long-term strategy for a public sector airline or steel company, for example, will be similar in many ways to one in the private sector. Nevertheless there are a number of respects in which the public sector enterprise is distinctive by the nature of its ownership.[1]

Purposes of State Ownership

It is wrong to approach the management of public sector enterprises as if they ought to be just the same as those in the private sector, and to regard any difference as an aberration. Public enterprises are frequently different, largely for the reasons which led to their being part of the public sector in the first place. These reasons are partly political and social, and partly to do with economics and efficiency.

The main political purpose of state ownership in the industrialised democracies has generally been a belief that the industry should be subject to a special measure of public control, and that public ownership is a more effective means of ensuring this than public regulation of a private enterprise. In many cases this belief reflected the fact that the industry in question provided a basic service to consumers and industries on a monopoly basis, for example, electricity or gas. It is thus unrealistic to imagine that such industries can be run with the same degree of managerial freedom as an ordinary private sector company.

The purpose of public ownership may also encompass the belief that any profits created by the enterprise should go into the public purse rather than private hands: the profits from distributing, if not producing, North Sea gas was a prime example. In such cases it is only reasonable that the government should take a close interest in the finances of the enterprise in question.

The relations between public enterprises of various kinds and the government itself is a recurring one in most countries with mixed economies, whether industrialised or developing. In India, for example, where state enterprise is particularly important in the manufacturing field, the emphasis on centralised planning of the economy for many years left very little scope for any strategic initiative by the enterprises themselves. At the other extreme, IRI, the Italian state holding company, was almost a law unto itself.

The economic purpose of state ownership has frequently been the integration or rationalisation of all (or at least a major part) of an industry into one unit. In the UK, integration was a major objective in bringing into public ownership the railways and also the generation and distribution of electricity. The rationalisation argument is somewhat different in nature. While the case for public ownership as a means of integration may be valid indefinitely, there may only be a need for rationalisation at a particular stage in the industry's development. Once the rationalisation has been achieved, the case for leaving the industry under unified management depends on such factors as economies of scale in production, marketing and research. In some cases a continuation of unified ownership may be advantageous; in others it may not.

The economic and political purposes of public ownership are frequently closely related. The economic factors which lead to monopoly (such as in the public utility field), by so doing, invite state ownership and control. Conversely, state ownership has itself tended to perpetuate the concentration of the industry into a single unit, whether or not this is an economic necessity. Recently, however, the arguments for breaking up monolithic state enterprises into separate units with some degree of competition have been broached, but the whole argument has been swamped in the politics of *privatisation*, i.e. a return to private ownership.[2]

There are a number of other factors which can lead to state ownership. One is dependence on government money for research and development, as in the aerospace and nuclear power industries. Another is dependence on government purchasing for military purposes. In addition, if an industry's problems are so severe as to lead to government intervention, this in turn may lead to state ownership, as happened with Rolls Royce or British Leyland. All these factors create special circumstances which may have a heavy influence on the strategic freedom of the management of the enterprise.

Where, however, state enterprises are operating more like 'ordinary' private sector companies, the practical impact of public ownership depends very much on the institutional and political framework in which they are operating — which may vary sharply from time to time. In Italy, for example, the state-owned steel industry shows strong public sector attributes when politically sensitive closures come on to the European Community agenda.

Forms of Public Ownership

'Public' ownership can take a variety of forms, which may be classified in four main groups.

The first is what might be termed the 'managerial corporation' or public utility, which is a form of public, but not government, ownership. The corporation is not run for the financial benefit of shareholders, but to supply a public service — as, for example, a harbour board or water board. These are generally loan-financed and 'non-profit-making' in the sense that there is no equity capital; but they differ from the 'nationalised industries' or municipal enterprises in that they are not owned and controlled by central or local government. Their boards may be composed in a number of ways, but they frequently contain representatives of what are regarded as the main interests involved, such as local authorities and business or individual consumers. They are 'managerial' in the sense that ultimate control rests with managers, in the form of the board, rather than with an owner, such as the state or equity shareholders.

The second type of public ownership is the 'departmental undertaking' of which the British Post Office was the prime example: that is, a public industry or service run as a government department. The employees are civil servants, and the Minister in charge of the department is the formal head of the undertaking. The finances of the undertaking are an integral part of the government's finances. A similar form is common in local authorities with local undertakings run by local government officers and responsible to a Committee of Councillors, with the Chairman of the Committee effectively Chairman of the undertaking. Examples are municipal halls and swimming baths. This type of organisation is the most political, and strategic management requires a high degree of political skill.

The third form of public ownership, long established in

France and Italy and growing in importance recently in the UK, is the company with a major state shareholding. Such a shareholding may give the government formal control because it has a shareholding ranging from 100 to 51 per cent; or it may leave it in an indeterminate position as the largest single shareholder, who may or may not wish to make use of that fact to control the company.

Finally there are the statutory public corporations, set up and governed by specific legislation, such as the 'nationalised industries' in the UK. These were set up by Act of Parliament, owned by central government, and their boards appointed by the Minister. Their basic constitutions followed the pattern set by the first nationalisation Acts under the 1945 Labour government. They provide a fascinating case study of the impact of political and institutional factors on strategic management.

Management Features

The four distinctive features of managing the UK nationalised industries are typical of many state enterprises. The first of these is close government control, partly a reflection of the statutory position in the nationalisation Acts, but also to a very important extent arising from the second factor, the industries' financial dependence on government. The third is the fact that they are generally large integrated organisations (see chapter 8) which require a particular style of management and a good deal of strategic planning. The fourth is their special obligations to consumers and the public.

The effect of these four factors on management varies from time to time and from country to country. The extent of government control varies widely; some public enterprises have access to private finance; their internal organisation differs considerably, as does the balance between strict commercialism and responsibility to the consuming public. But to some extent or other these four factors are an inescapable feature of public ownership.

Relations with Government

Relations with government are bound to be a major element in the work of top management in the public sector; this is a natural corollary of the initial legislation in the case of statutory authorities. Formally, the government's powers over management as laid down by the nationalisation Acts were not blanket powers in the same way as those of the owners of a company in the private sector. They were originally defined with the intention of limiting the government's powers to intervene in day-to-day matters, and hence absolve it from answering to Parliament for the detailed running of the corporations (as used to be the case with the Post Office when it was a government department). But the fact that the government appoints the Chairman and Board and is the sole source of finance effectively gives it unrestricted control over the industries. The extent to which it uses this power depends very much on the circumstances of the moment.

A typical nationalisation Act has four key provisions, covering: the duties of the corporation; the powers of the corporation; the powers of the Secretary of State; and financial provisions.

To take the British Steel Corporation (now privatised) as an example, its original *duties* were to promote the efficient and economical supply of steel (these were subsequently modified to allow it to cease production of particular products which it regarded as unprofitable). It must not exercise unfair discrimination, and it must promote exports and research. The *Corporation's powers* were to produce and sell steel. It could hold interests in other companies only with the consent of the Secretary of State.

The *powers of the Secretary of State* included that of giving 'general directions'. Although this was a blanket power included in the various statutes, it was virtually never used; but its existence constituted a deterrent which has made effective the so-called 'lunchtime directive': i.e. the informal request from the Minister to the Chairman of the Board, generally 'an offer he can't refuse'. The Minister was also required to approve the Corporation's general programme of investment, and, in the case of the BSC, proposals for the organisation of the Corporation.

The *financial provisions* of the Act required the Corporation to borrow from the government or with the approval of the Secretary of State and the Treasury. In addition, a limit to the total borrowing powers of the Corporation was set by Parliament and required Parliamentary approval when it was raised. The Treasury could guarantee borrowing by the Corporation, a power mainly used when the Corporations were encouraged to borrow on the Eurodollar market for balance of payments reasons.

Operation of Government Control

The practical operation of government control reflects to some extent the strength or weakness of the financial position of the industry. Industries making losses or requiring large sums for investment tend to come under more stringent control than those in a more independent financial position, although at times the more profitable industries, such as gas or electricity, may get enmeshed in the government's fund-raising activities.

The industries' need to get approval for their investment programmes up to three to five years' ahead is one of the principal means by which the government exercises control over their strategy. This reflects the fact that most of the industries are capital-intensive and the scale and nature of their investment programme is a reflection of the strategy they are planning to follow. In addition, the government may also exercise control over individual major projects (a power generally attributable to its powers over the investment programmes rather than any specific statutory provision). The size and type of project over which this control is exercised varies from industry to industry and from time to time, but it provides the government with a further means of questioning the strategies being followed by the Corporations.

In the UK the major instrument of financial control in the 1980s was the imposition of annual borrowing limits:

External Financing Limits (EFL). These are based on cash-flow forecasts submitted to Government and are intended to influence both the Corporations' operating results and their capital investment. To take a simple example:

	£ million
Profit/loss	+ 112
less Increase in working capital	− 17
less Fixed investment	− 165
Other capital transactions	+ 2
Borrowing requirement (EFL)	− 68

The problem with this form of control is that the profit or loss is difficult to forecast and is only to a limited extent capable of being determined by management in the short run, whereas expenditure on fixed investment cannot be speedily adjusted, as much of the expenditure on major projects in any particular year is on projects already under way. When economic conditions are deteriorating and operating results are worse than forecast, adjustments tend to fall either on stocks or on fixed investment, as the system permits no contingency allowances for shortfalls in profits in determining borrowing limits (unlike the arrangements a private firm would normally make with its bank for overdraft facilities).

Other instruments of government control, set out in successive White Papers on the Nationalised Industries, include the *Test Discount Rate* (TDR) and more recently the *Required Rate of Return* (RRR).[3] The TDR is the cut-off point for the discounted cash-flow return ('internal rate of return') on a project. Each industry needs such a cut-off point for its own internal management purposes. The White Papers set this at a common level (first 8 per cent in real terms, then 10 per cent) for all industries, on the basis that this was the level attainable by companies in the private sector. The difficulties of relating such a rate to the return the industries were actually getting on their assets as a whole led to the introduction of a concept intermediate between the TDR and the accounting concept of net return on assets: namely, the *Required Rate of Return* (originally 5 per cent, but raised in 1989 to 8 per cent in real terms) on the industry's new investment looking at the investment programme as a whole. There has, however, been difficulty in making this effective because of the problems of determining the increase in profits attributable to an investment programme comprising a variety of projects starting and finishing at different dates.

The more orthodox concept of *Financial Targets*, in the form of the rate of return on net assets, has provided an easier yardstick by which to judge financial results and discuss medium-term plans. It provides no solution, however, to the more basic problem of what to do if an industry consistently fails to meet its targets.

Strategic Constraints

State industries fall into two main groups. The first consists of those that are primarily public utilities. They tend to be statutory monopolies and, because of the nature of their products, are not subject to foreign competition: electricity, gas, water, docks, airports, posts, telecommunications, railways. Industries in the second group may or may not have a complete monopoly of national production, but they are subject to foreign competition (often intense) and operate in world markets: for example, airways, steel, shipbuilding and to some extent coal. The problems of the second group are most akin to those of planning in the large private sector companies. Both groups, however, are subject to tighter constraints than those experienced in the private sector.

Fields of Activity

The first major constraint arises when the field of activity of the public corporation (that is, the industry in which it is to operate) is laid down by statute, and the scope for diversification is heavily restricted both by statutory control and by the effects of political pressures. There is little point in the strategist posing the question, 'What business are we in?' The answer is laid down by law. (This was the position for the UK nationalised industries.) Diversification strategies are virtually impossible to pursue for a number of reasons. There is first the feeling that the industry has enough to do managing its core business without getting involved in peripheral activities. There is also pressure on government not to allow state-financed industries to compete with established industries in other fields, and government reluctance to make additional capital available for this purpose. The degree of difficulty has depended on the political complexion of the government in power, but the lowest common denominator has tended to be the determining factor, because the corporations are naturally reluctant to embark on a long-term strategy of diversification under one government that might bring it into the forefront of political controversy and make it liable to reversal with a change in government.

Market Share

The attitude of a nationalised industry to market share as a strategic factor is frequently different from that of a private sector company. The public utilities tend to have a monopoly in their own product, although they may be competing in a wider market, as are gas and electricity in the total market for energy. Those subject to international competition are generally fighting for market share in the home market and other markets; they still see themselves as leaders in the home market, and their strategic decisions about market share arise mainly in determining export strategies.

Methods of Financing

In the UK all long-term finance for the nationalised industries (with the exception of government-encouraged Eurodollar borrowing) has come from the Treasury (National Loans Fund). It has consisted almost entirely of fixed interest debt, with just a modicum of government-held equity in the form of *Public Dividend Capital* for one or two industries. The room to manoeuvre in determining possible financial strategies is hence severely limited.

Pricing Policy

The pricing policy of publicly owned utilities is heavily subject to government influence − both downwards and upwards. At certain times the pressure has been to keep prices down as part of a general attempt to limit price increases; at other times nationalised industries such as electricity and gas have been compelled to raise prices to reduce the *Public Sector Borrowing Requirement* (PSBR). The fact that the pricing policy of these industries is significant in macroeconomic terms is bound to make them susceptible to government intervention for such purposes. This does not arise in the case of industries such as steel, facing international price competition, whose room to manoeuvre is strongly limited by market forces.

Pay

Wage and salary negotiations in such industries are often subject to much greater government influence than the private sector and to considerable behind-the-scenes intervention. This reflects the fear that major industries in the public sector will set the lead in the pay round, and is partly a consequence of the publicity their pay negotiations attract. It is also a measure of the widespread consequences (both economic and political) of industrial disputes in many of these industries.

Social Pressures

State industries are particularly subject to social pressures − indeed, that was often one of the objectives of nationalisation. Very often this pressure is not direct, but comes through the government, which in turn is concerned about the reaction of particular pressure groups or electoral considerations. The standards of social responsibility expected from the nationalised industries are greater than for the private sector. This applies not just on special issues, such as disconnecting consumers who have not paid their gas or electricity bills, but also on subjects like redundancies and closures. The closure of pits and steelworks has been a direct concern of government in a way that closure of private sector plant of similar size has not.

The Need for Government Agreement

Finally, the most important constraint of all is the need for public corporations to secure government agreement to any effective strategy. The problem is not necessarily that the government actually disagrees with the industry's proposed strategy, but that it may not want to be publicly committed to it (or any other overt statement of intent that might prove politically embarrassing). It then becomes very difficult for the industry to pursue its preferred strategy without the necessary government backing.

Apart from the political factors making governments hesitant to agree on a strategy, the civil service mechanism of control is often directed at the public expenditure aspects of the corporations' activities, in particular at figures for future profits and investment expenditure, rather than the strategy and strategic objectives determining the financial results. Moreover, the figures which command most attention are those for the year ahead and the consequent borrowing requirement. The government's interest tends to be essentially short-term and the machinery of government unconducive to any stable agreement between the government and the nationalised industries on long-term strategy.

Political Uncertainty

Political uncertainty is a particular factor to which the management of these industries must be sensitive. It is not just a matter of possible changes in government every four or five years; the Minister responsible for an industry may change at much shorter intervals. Just as one Minister has become familiar with, and possibly sympathetic to, the problems of the industry, he moves on, and the Chairman has to begin again to establish a new working relationship with the next Minister.

The most inhibiting form of uncertainty in a corporation's relations with government concerns the position of the organisation itself: whether, for example, it is to be re-organised or privatised. Anything that threatens an organisational upheaval naturally tends to become a major preoccupation of top management of the organisation. The situation is analogous to a take-over bid in the private sector, except that the disturbance may go on for years rather than weeks or months.

Quantitative Forecasting

While strategic issues take on a much more political aspect in the public sector, many of the key strategic decisions in these industries are quantitative; in particular, they are concerned with the tonnage of coal required, the amount of generating capacity, the volume of steel capacity. Because these industries are producing in large quantities, and have only a limited range of products, strategic issues frequently revolve around the volume of capacity and output and hence the number of jobs involved – particularly in times of depression. Quantitative forecasting of demand thus becomes a key feature in the formulation of strategy. These forecasts are generally closely bound up with the uncertainties about general macroeconomic developments, because the products involved tend to be widely consumed and demand for them depends on the general state of the economy. The only way to deal with the never-ending problem of uncertainty is to examine carefully the implications of differing forecasts of the key variables for the policies under consideration. Yet so great is the pressure to keep things simple and stick to one set of numbers, that inadequate examination of the effects of varying such forecasts is the most common weakness in strategic planning in this field.

Strategy in the Public Sector

Strategic issues for state enterprises are thus in some ways simpler and in other ways more complex than for the large private sector company. They may be simpler in that their room for manoeuvre is much more limited: in terms of diversification, market share, closures and very often pricing and pay. They are more complex in that there are more interested parties to be consulted or convinced before any strategy can be adopted: primarily the government itself, but also members of Parliament, parliamentary committees, trade unions, consumer bodies and local authorities – all of which are more active, and have more effective power, in relation to public sector industry than private. A successful and viable strategy must command sufficient support from these various interested parties to remain stable for long enough to be made effective.

Public Utilities

The process of privatisation of many of the former nationalised industries in the UK has highlighted the distinction between (a) state ownership of enterprises in essentially competitive industries, like aerospace and steel and (b) public utilities like the railways, gas, electricity and water. The more ardent advocates of privatisation appear to take the view that public utilities can be run just like any other company, except that they may need a regulating body to ensure that they do not overcharge the public. This has meant that even where there have been, for example, privately owned water companies, these have not been taken as the models for privatisation; rather it has been assumed that privatised utilities will be basically the same as any other private sector company. This is unrealistic. It ignores both historical experience in the UK and the evidence of other countries.

Public utilities inevitably have a distinctive ethos – water is the most obvious example. Water companies supply a basic necessity for which there is no substitute product and consumers have no choice but to obtain their water from the local monopoly supplier. Security of supply and hygienic standards are expected to be paramount. The concept of profit maximisation is not generally acceptable: the financial objective is almost universally regarded as being to meet demand as efficiently as possible and make an adequate, but not exceptional, return on capital. A public utility's primary responsibility is to the public rather than its owners. Water supply is a public utility *par excellence*, so are the railways. The organisation is there to supply a need, subject to financial constraints, *not* to make the maximum profit subject to meeting certain social obligations.

Strategy formulation and strategic planning for public utilities, even though 'privately' owned is in many ways more akin to that in state enterprises than ordinary private sector companies. First, the basic product and market are inexorably determined. Second, the strategy must start from considering public demand and how to meet it *in full*. Third, the competition, if any, will generally come from alternative forms of fuel or transport rather than other organisations supplying the same product – telecommunications is the most obvious exception to this. Fourth, strategy is almost inevitably concerned with very long-term factors. Fifth, strategy must pay particular attention to the views of central and local government. Finally the utilities must always bear in mind the possible reaction of their official regulator to their proposed plans.

Regulation is a major fact of life for public utilities: not only price control, but also control over pricing policy in such matters as price discrimination and the structure of tariffs, and sometimes more general control over other aspects of policy. Price control adds a further dimension to investment evaluation. The forecasting problem is complicated by uncertainty not merely as to what prices could be charged but also as to what prices the firm will be *allowed* to charge. From one point of view price control might be regarded as something of a cushion with the expectation that whatever the precise formula adopted, the regulators will tend to validate past investment decisions by allowing the utility a reasonable return on its assets. While, however, it is often alleged that regulators get 'captured' by the industries they are meant to control, the reverse can also happen. Conflict between the regulators and the industry can develop a 'macho' element, with the regulators anxious to demonstrate their virility by holding down prices. The Iron and Steel Board followed such an energetic price control policy in the 1960s based on greenfield site plant costs that when the industry was nationalised it was only earning a 1 per cent return on capital.

There is thus an inevitable tendency for enterprises with long lead-times such as in electricity generation, to seek formal or informal validation of their major investment decisions from the regulatory authority in the hope that this will increase the chances that subsequent prices will be set at a level that will provide an adequate return. This is particularly important where investment is directed at increasing capacity, improving quality or reducing pollution (as in the case of water) rather than at reducing costs. Similarly in a fragmented or partially competitive field like electricity generation, the regulators themselves will find it difficult to avoid taking an interest in firms' investment plans. If these are inadequate, total demand will not be met (the public's first requirement). If investment is excessive there will eventually be problems about prices and profitability.

It would thus be wrong to think that private ownership of public utilities, with the necessary concomitant of regulatory offices, will leave the management with the same freedom of manoeuvre as the ordinary company. In place of their former control by government departments, they will face a new and in some respects more negative control from the regulators. Thus both the process of formulating strategy and its content will eventually tend to bear a closer relation to that of state-owned enterprises than might be imagined at first sight.

Notes

1 For a general review see John Grieve Smith (ed.), *Strategic Planning in Nationalised Industries*, 1984.
2 M. Beesley and S. Littlechild, 'Privatisation: Principles, Problems and Priorities', *Lloyds Bank Review*, July 1983.
3 Nationalised Industries White Papers: 1961 (Cmnd 1337); 1967 (Cmnd 3437) and 1978 (Cmnd 7131).

11

Small, High-technology Firms

Explicit strategies and formal planning are more frequently associated with large firms than small ones. But knowing where you want to go and how you intend to get there can be as important to a small firm as a large one. This applies particularly to new firms set up to develop new products, or processes, and hoping to achieve rapid growth. This chapter discusses the strategic problems of small, high-technology companies.[1] In recent years such companies have received a good deal of publicity, particularly those visibly associated with local universities through Science Parks; but companies of a similar nature have existed for many years: particularly in the scientific instrument industry.

In the early stages of a firm's development, the founders' objectives for the firm tend to be closely bound up with their own personal objectives in starting it. This is particularly true in the financial field. If their prime objective is to be independent and work for themselves, they may be wary of outside investment because they feel it may threaten or weaken their control over the business. On the other hand, if their prime objective (perhaps because of age) is to build up the value of the business and then sell out, they may be more enthusiastic about outside equity investment in the company (e.g. by a Venture Capital company). So the first need is to clarify the personal objectives of the founder or founders. These should cover such points as: where does he or she want to live and work; are they prepared to commit all their personal capital to the business; are they looking for immediate returns; are they prepared to share responsibility with managers recruited from outside; are they trying to avoid, or to secure, a take-over by a larger firm?

Where the firm is to be founded by more than one

person (e.g. a group of colleagues) it is important that they should reach the necessary degree of agreement on such objectives. If they do not, there may be irreconcilable tensions from the start. Certainly, when the personal objectives of the founders diverge, the firm will tend to split. Much of the fissioning of such companies seems to reflect the conflicting personal objectives of the key individuals involved.

A further key area where prior agreement is needed, but sometimes seems lacking, is over the particular roles of the individuals involved. Ideally the founders of a small firm should have differing interests, skills and backgrounds, but very often they come together as friends or colleagues with similar interests and experiences. It is then particularly important that before they start up they should clarify who is to look after particular aspects of the business and, if it is of any size, who is to be Chairman, who Managing Director, etc. Above all, the strategy chosen must be matched to the skills and experience of the founders.

The founders of new high-technology firms have generally been intimately concerned with the development of the technology on which the products of their new firm are to be based, probably working in a university or research institute laboratory. Their personal financial stake in the new company is often financed by remortgaging their house. The remaining finance may come from a variety of sources, but almost certainly will include some borrowing from a bank. At this stage they will need a 'business plan' to show potential investors. But while the discipline of preparing such a plan can be a useful one, there is also a danger in constructing sales and cash-flow forecasts for three or four years when the products to be sold are not yet finally developed. A prior and more basic need is to clarify the fundamental objectives and approach of the firm.

Formulating Strategy

Product and Market Strategy

The most basic strategic question of all is: What is the company going to sell? Product strategy and financial strategy are clearly interrelated. Capital requirements depend on the choice of product, and conversely the introduction of new products must be related to the capital available. The capital required depends on:

1 the time and resources required to develop and test the new product;
2 the investment to produce it;
3 the investment in marketing and distribution;
4 the time needed to build up sales and production to a break-even level.

British biotechnology companies provide diverse examples of the effects of the amount of capital initially available on the product strategies adopted.

The major British biotechnology company Celltech is a comparatively rare example of a new company raising a large amount of initial capital and going straight for an ambitious product option. These tend to be companies with some institutional parentage or backing. Celltech was founded in 1980 by the National Enterprise Board and the Medical Research Council, in partnership with four financial institutions, with an original equity capital of £12 million. By 1987, it had raised a total of £23 million through equity placing. The availability of finance on this scale enabled it to instal its own production facilities and see its ultimate role as a full scale pharmaceutical company.

The Agricultural Genetics Company (AGC) founded in 1983, was also founded with official blessing, but its initial funding was on a much smaller scale and its strategy necessarily less ambitious. It started by sub-contracting research from large companies to government and university labs to generate short-term cash from management fees. But in a third round of financing in 1984, it raised £15 million and was in a position to start developing its own product lines, such as human growth hormone.

Some companies have devised stratagems to enable them to start up with the minimum of finance. Cambridge Research Biochemicals (CRB) started in 1980 with an initial capital of £12,000, relabelling and distributing the peptides of an American company, Biochem. By 1982 several peptides were in great demand, so the company began to manufacture these itself. Later in its development, CRB raised £1 million in an equity/licensing deal with Millipore who were looking for an overseas distributor for their peptide synthesis instruments. Eventually CRB sold out to ICI.

The changes in a firm's product-mix over time will tend to reflect the process of what may be termed '*product progression*'. By this we mean a strategy of starting at the bottom end of the range of capital intensity (i.e. with products or activities minimising capital requirements) and then, as the firm develops, moving up to the more ambitious products with greater capital requirements. The initial 'product' for many embryonic high-technology firms is consultancy. This requires little or no capital and generates a relatively speedy cash-flow. Another 'product' which keeps down capital requirements is contract Research and Development. In the case of new biotechnology firms their early products may be standard products such as monoclonal cell lines or peptides for other larger producers or specialised products produced under contract; or they may undertake contract research. The next more elaborate group of products includes diagnostic kits of various types for use with humans or animals. Then come drugs for animal use and, finally, and most demanding in terms of capital, drugs for human use.

The different groups of products are not necessarily mutually exclusive: many firms will be selling products at more than one stage in the progression at any given time. But they will tend to start with a product portfolio concentrated at the lower end of the range and move towards one with higher proportions of the more elaborate and capital demanding products as the firms develop.

Such a progression in terms of capital requirements is conceptually distinct from the development of technically more advanced products in response to the product life cycle — although both factors are likely to be at work simultaneously as the product-mix of a firm changes over time. The more elaborate products introduced as capital becomes more plentiful may, or may not, embody technology partially developed in earlier, simpler products: some of the initial products may be simply a diversion to generate cash. But a well-integrated development strategy will be concerned both with the continual modernisation of product lines and with developing a more ambitious and capital-intensive product-mix to match the growth of the firm's capital resources.

Financial Strategy

Two key elements in financial strategy are:

1 the magnitude and timing of capital requirements
2 the desired, or acceptable ratio of borrowing to equity finance

The typical small, new company will start with a small amount of capital from the founders, a bank loan and possibly some further start-up finance from a financial institution. The next step will be to raise additional capital from further loans and by placing equity with a limited number of investing institutions. Succeeding rounds of finance may follow a similar pattern until the company reaches a point where it is ready for a public flotation or its financing requirements are resolved by a take-over by a larger company.

The main sources of finance for new firms are:

1 the founder or founders (and sometimes their relations and friends);
2 the clearing banks;
3 other financial institutions (e.g. insurance companies and pension funds);
4 Venture Capital Funds;
5 private or public institutions specialising in providing capital for small firms, in particular in the UK 3i's (Investors in Industry);
6 government schemes to assist small or high-technology firms.

In addition firms may raise money by mortgaging property or leasing plant and equipment.

With the exception of the clearing banks (who will only provide loans or overdrafts), these various sources may provide either equity or loan finance, or a combination of the two. The amount of finance that the firm is able or prepared to raise will be a key factor in the strategy to be adopted; so too will be the proportion of equity and the expectations of its providers.

When it comes to raising outside finance, the founders of the business are typically torn between their desire to maintain control by keeping a majority of the equity in their own hands and the desire of other institutions to take an equity stake in the company as well as providing loan capital. The relative proportions of debt and equity capital that are acceptable either to the firm or suppliers of finance depend partly on the riskiness of the business and partly on the lead-time before products are available on the market. In some fields (e.g. biotechnology) long lead-times in development make reliance on loan capital impractical and substantial amounts of equity essential. Moreover, in such cases the equity has to be provided on the understanding that no dividends will be paid for some years. Most new biotechnology companies' expenditure on R and D is greater than any profits from operations in their early years and they therefore show overall losses for some time. Such firms are highly dependant on their ability to raise equity, but to do so they need a convincing strategy for their future development.

On the other hand some high-technology firms have managed to finance their initial development almost entirely from loans, particularly scientific instrument makers. An example from a wider field is Domino Printing Sciences. Domino was formed in 1978 to exploit ink jet printing technology. It started with £50,000 capital from its founder, Graeme Minto, together with a loan of £25,000 from Cambridge Consultants Ltd, and its early growth was mainly financed by a series of further loans from 3i's (Investors in Industry) until its flotation in 1985 which raised a net £2.7 million.

Domino's ability to finance itself in its early years by taking on such a heavy burden of loan capital reflected the following factors:

1 It developed a saleable product and went into profit relatively quickly. After losses of just over £100,000 in its first two years, it made a small profit in the third.
2 Staff and expenses were kept to a minimum in the initial period.
3 Fixed capital requirements (apart from buildings) were low and largely financed by hire-purchase.
4 The assembly nature of the operation and the terms negotiated with suppliers and distributors or customers limited working capital requirements.
5 The rapid expansion of the company reduced the burden of interest payments as a proportion of profits from 18 per cent in 1981–2 to 7 per cent in 1983–4.

The success of the company then made possible a public flotation and a switch to equity financing for the next stage of its expansion.

Manufacturing Strategy

One of the key decisions facing many new companies is the extent to which they should manufacture their products themselves as opposed to relying on sub-contractors. New electronic companies, for example, have tended to concentrate on the assembly and testing of bought-in components; whereas many older instrument companies regard themselves as straightforward manufacturers. It is quite usual for companies selling new high-technology products to limit their own commitment to manufacturing. There is the best of precedents. Henry Ford started his first automobile production by assembling sub-contracted chassis and components.

Reliance on sub-contractors minimises the firm's own capital requirements. It can then concentrate its available capital on financing activities which it must do itself, such as product development and sales. Moreover, the majority of new high-technology entrepreneurs have no experience of manufacturing. Many firms would also claim that by avoiding investment in facilities dedicated to the production of particular products they preserve a greater degree of flexibility to abandon old products and switch to new ones.

An extreme variant of this approach is to purchase computer hardware and add specialised software. An important part of the product may then be the installation of the system, staff training and subsequent service and maintenance – as, for example, has been the policy of a computer-aided design company such as Cambridge Interactive Systems.

A further incentive for European and North American companies to buy-in hardware is the low cost of products from South-east Asia and more generally the ability to switch purchases to whatever may be the lowest cost source at the time. This was, for example, the policy followed very successfully by Amstrad in building up its personal computer business.

Avoiding involvement in manufacturing may, however, weaken a firm's control over the quality of its product. Hence once a firm has become established the question of undertaking its own manufacturing tends to be re-opened. In the case of new biotechnology companies this is a particularly serious problem as there is not generally an infrastructure of sub-contractors available to meet their requirements. Hence a major strategic decision is whether to extend into manufacture. On a recent visit to two US biotechnology firms, I found one, (Praxis) had taken a decision to set up a manufacturing plant in North Carolina with the help of regional development incentives. Another smaller firm was in a state of crisis because the Chairman had just been out-voted by the Board, having failed to persuade them to invest in their own manufacturing facilities after five joint manufacturing ventures had failed.

Research and Development

Almost by definition, the lifeblood of high-technology companies is their research and development effort. Research gave them their original *raison d'être* and the development of saleable new products is basic to their success. The concept of the 'product life cycle' (see chapter 4) is closely associated with high-technology products, where there tends to be rapid development of successive products. (It should not, however, be assumed that high technology always means a short life cycle. Nuclear power is a good example to the contrary. The Pressurized Water Reactor, for example, has been in use for over 30 years.) Nevertheless, rapid change is a keynote over much of this field and it is generally necessary for such firms to plan in terms of continual development of their products, with older products dropping out and new ones being introduced. Hence the firm must have a strategy which not only encompasses its ability to produce and sell its immediate range of products, but also the ability to develop, produce and sell its successors. The R and D effort is a vital part of this.

Small, high-technology firms show a variety of approaches to R and D policy. At the most modest end of the spectrum is the firm, such as an instrument-maker, which is selling a product developed in co-operation with a customer (in this case a university laboratory) and quietly refining and improving it in a gradual way. At the more ambitious end of the spectrum is the biotechnology firm with a substantial R and D effort which represents a very substantial investment (albeit for accounting purposes treated as current operating costs). In the latter case there is a heavy financial burden and probably a long lead-time from the start of R and D expenditure to the sale of a viable product. The scope and direction of such an R and D programme must be closely geared to the firm's product and financial strategies.

Of course, R and D can itself be a product. A small company wishing to employ a more expensive R and D team than it can itself support in the short term may still contract R and D to other firms. (The reverse of a small company contracting out some of its R and D to a larger firm is less likely.)

Manpower and Management

Small firms naturally tend to have a more personal flavour than large ones. But in the high-technology case, the technological knowledge, expertise and ability of the key management are (initially at any rate) the firm's most important and distinctive assets. It is therefore crucial to make the best use of these human resources. So even before the firm is off the ground, it needs a basic 'strategy' for the founding management, defining the respective roles of its founding members. This must identify: the basic tasks of management; the abilities, experience and predelictions of the founders and the gaps (and sometimes surpluses) left. One of the keys to success is to recognise the limitations of the original management and take steps to make good its shortcomings by suitable outside recruitment – often of an experienced general manager in a related industry. An advantage of involvement with Venture Capital companies, or financial institutions, is that they are very keen on getting this right. Failure to sort this out is a major source of conflict and the break-up of companies as they develop.

As the firm develops, its organisation must change both in response to changes in the number employed and to the balance of different types of activity. Hence in recruiting individuals who it is hoped will stay with it during its successful expansion, it is wise to pay some heed to these prospective changes. Initially the new high-technology firm with a small, high-powered staff is likely to have an informal and loosely defined organisation. But as it grows, its organisation will need a greater degree of formality with jobs and reporting relationships more explicitly defined. The need for effective financial controls will work in the same direction. At the same time, an increase in the relative importance of sales and production activities will create the need for more conventional management structures.

Firms with a clear will to expand need to pay as much or more attention to their management development and manpower strategy as any other branch of strategic thinking. Whereas the products to be produced five years hence are probably not yet on the drawing board, most of the people in the firm today will still be there.

Relationships with Large Firms

One of the most difficult problems for the small high-technology firm is that of managing its relationships with larger firms. These may involve licensing agreements, long-term contracts, joint ventures or other arrangements to help the smaller firm develop, produce or sell its products in one way or another. The small firm very often needs something which the large firm has got, and it has not; but the imbalance of power between them makes it difficult to ensure that their relationship remains beneficial to the small partner.

The most common need for a link with a large firm arises on the sales side. Sometimes it stems from the fact that the large company, such as a major computer firm, constitutes a major market for a smaller producer of specialised equipment. The risks of such dependence are fairly obvious and long-term agreements may still leave the small supplier vulnerable, unless it can make itself indispensable. In some fields, the relationship with the large firm hinges on the fact that it has the distribution facilities the small one lacks. This often applies to a biotechnology firm selling medical products.

An example of such an alliance is the relation between the young American company, Praxis Biologics, and the established pharmaceutical firm, Bristol-Meyers. The latter helped finance the new company in two ways. It bought stock in the company; and it made substantial payments to help finance the development of certain vaccines in exchange for exclusive distribution rights in North America. This substantial assistance, however, did place the smaller firm in a vulnerable position. Bristol-Meyers had the right to decline to make future payments for any product in return for forfeiting distribution rights. Moreover, in the case of three vaccines, Bristol-Meyers had the right to determine the final selling price and pay Praxis a fixed percentage of that price.[2]

UK firms are often in particular need of a distributor in the US which is generally the largest, single market for high-technology products. Such a relationship frequently leads to a take-over. Cambridge Interactive Systems had a distribution arrangement in the US with Prime Computers, who then attempted an unwelcome take-over which led to an eventual take-over by another American firm, Computervision. On the other hand, Domino acquired its

American licensee and distributor in an endeavour to tackle problems at that end.

The problem for the small firm is to strike up a relationship which does not imperil its future by leaving excessive power with its larger partner. The strength of the small firm depends mainly on its technological expertise being valuable to the large firm and not easily obtainable elsewhere. It is generally in the nature of such relationships that the smaller partner can have only one large partner of this kind. The smaller firm's vulnerability rests partly on the danger of the large firm breaking off the agreement and leaving it without a major market or its main distributor. Vulnerability also arises from agreements which leave the major party a dominant voice over crucial factors, like the volume or price. It is essential for the small firm to look at the management style and track record of any potential partner to assess the chances of an even-handed future relationship. It is also vital to consider very carefully the detailed provisions of any such agreements.

For their part, large companies need to take a broad strategic view of their relationships with small companies pioneering in new technological fields. The strategy of many pharmaceutical companies has been to wait on the sidelines while the new, small firms make the running in biotechnology. In that case there is a great deal to be said for systematically cultivating relationships with such firms, some of which will come to nothing, but some of which may prove extremely valuable in the long run. It would seem that for the very large company in, say, pharmaceuticals or electronics, positive encouragement of those pioneering new technologies would be both statesmanlike and ultimately beneficial. There is, however, very little evidence of leading firms (in the UK at any rate) adopting such far-sighted policies. They seem rather to make short-term tactical acquisitions from time to time as circumstances dictate.

Strategic Guidelines

It is important for new and growing high-technology firms

to have a clear strategy, albeit one sufficiently flexible to adapt to changing circumstances. This must give *consistent* answers to a number of closely related questions.

1 What are to be the firm's initial products and how is it intending to develop its product-mix?
2 Where and to whom are its products to be sold?
3 How are these products to be sold and distributed? Is the firm relying on its own sales force, agents, distributors or agreements with larger firms?
4 To what extent is the firm producing the products itself or relying on sub-contractors?
5 What are its R and D objectives and what resources will these require?
6 What staff will be required and how will these be organised?
7 What are the implications for cash-flow and profitability? What are the capital requirements; and in what form and by whom are they to be supplied?

To answer these questions consistently will require some form of business plan, particularly to assess the financial implications. But the key requirement is to have clear answers to the basic policy issues. The numbers, albeit an essential discipline, are bound to be subject to a large measure of uncertainty and thus to some extent indicative. Hence while the answers to question seven on financial strategy initially interact with those to the earlier questions, once a limited amount of finance has been obtained it may then become a constraint to which the answers to questions one to six need to be adjusted tactically. But the inevitable uncertainty about financial requirements should, so far as possible, be explicitly recognised both by the firm and its financial supporters.

Notes

1 The joint research on which this chapter is based is discussed in more detail in three articles by Vivien Fleck and the author: 'Business Strategies in Small High-Technology

Companies', *Long Range Planning*, April 1987; 'Strategies of New Biotechnology Firms', *Long Range Planning*, June 1988; and 'Strategy and Finance in Small High-Technology Companies', in Aubrey Silberston (ed.), *Technology and Economic Progress*, Macmillan, 1988.
2 Prospectus for the sale of 1,750,000 shares in Praxis Biologics, 27 March 1987, Shearson Lehman Brothers Inc. and Merrill Lynch Capital Markets.

12

People and Change

Three themes have received particular attention in recent writing on strategic management: first, that changes in the business environment have become more rapid and un-expected; second, that top management is, and should be, increasingly concerned with non-economic objectives; third, that there has been a reaction against the 'rational' or analytical approach to decision-making. All these themes have an element of truth in them, but they also contain a number of misconceptions and need to be put into proper perspective.

Increasing Turbulence?

Ansoff, the progenitor of the doctrine of increasing tur-bulence asserts that during the twentieth century changes in the environment have become progressively faster, more novel and more difficult to anticipate.[1] His concept of in-creasing 'turbulence' first gained prominence after the oil crises in the early 1970s which led to the break-down of the post-war period of economic expansion, 25 years of growth and stability. The emphasis on increasing turbulence seems timely again at the start of the 1990s with dramatic and revolutionary changes taking place in Eastern Europe and the Soviet Union. But looking at these events in the longer context of a century of dramatic political events, inter-spersed with two world wars, they seem more a continuation of an unfolding series than a completely new departure.

Whatever may be said about the speed of political change, however, the suggestion that the impact of tech-nological change is accelerating is highly debatable.

Look at the world around us. Transport is one of the

most fundamental influences in our social and industrial life. We have been living in the age of the motor car for seventy years. The jet airliner has been with us for thirty years and its arrival was foreshadowed for fifteen years by the use of the jet engine in military aircraft. We have been dominated by television for over thirty years. The computer is perhaps the most significant recent innovation − but it has been with us for twenty-five years.

Faced with the thesis of increasing turbulence, I often compare the changes in my own lifetime with those of my grandmother born into the Victorian Age. She lived through the building of the railway network and the introduction of widespread rail travel: the invention and mass production of the motor car: the invention of the aeroplane and the spread of air travel: the introduction of vacuum cleaners, refrigerators, radio and television: two world wars: the atom bomb and nuclear power. Admittedly, she lived to be 101. But as a true product of the Victorian Age she relished it all. (Her greatest regret was that she never went up in an aeroplane.) Even if we live as long, will we be able to cap such a catalogue of technological and social change? I doubt it.

Technological change since the Second World War has not in fact been very sudden or unexpected. One reason for this is that, as technology becomes more complex, more work is needed to develop new processes, lead-times lengthen and, even though success or failure may not be predictable, the possibilities ahead become known well in advance. The development of nuclear power and space travel, perhaps the two most sensational developments of our time, will probably prove to have a twenty-five to fifty year lead-time from initial conception to widespread utilisation.

Similarly, in the economic field, the 1929 financial crisis and ensuing depression was more traumatic and had more disastrous consequences, both in the industrialised countries and among primary commodity producers, than the 1980s world depression.

Nor, in the political field, has change become consistently faster: it has remained erratic. By historical standards the period from 1945 to the late 1980s was one of relative stability. The previous thirty years saw the Bolshevik revolution, the rise of Stalin and Hitler, the Second World War. In the postwar period, the only political developments of comparable magnitude were the granting of independence to the countries comprising the former British Empire, a long foreseen and inevitable development, and the absorption of Eastern Europe into the Russian empire.

The 1989 revolutions in Eastern Europe and the break-up of the Russian empire follow 40 years of remarkably little political change. Now, however, moves towards a more liberal economic and political system in the Soviet Union seem likely to have a major impact on the volume and nature of its trade with the West. Liberalisation in Eastern Europe and the end of Soviet domination there may erode the harsh political division of Europe between East and West with consequences, as yet unacknowledged, for the European Community. The easing of tension seems likely to lead to substantial cuts in armament expenditure by both East and West with significant and widespread economic ramifications, particularly from the two major powers. Such changes should, however, not take companies unawares as they are being signalled some years ahead.

Coping with Change

The problem is not that change has become more rapid, or more uncertain in direction. It is rather that we are losing our appetite for change as the possibilities of change become more threatening. At any rate, certain groups in society feel this way. Certainly the widespread adoption of nuclear weapons constitutes a threat to civilised life of unprecedented severity. Terrorism has become a part of everyday life in most parts of the world. The maintenance of democratic conditions even in the United States and United Kingdom can no longer be taken for granted. The threat of *adverse* change has now become more fearful.

In addition, in the field of industrial management, the more elaborate and settled organisations that we now have, with a greater expectation of personal security, are less susceptible to change. Current norms of behaviour make it difficult to sack workers or managers at will in the face of changing market conditions as was possible fifty years ago – and the changing social ethos has made it much more unpleasant for the individual manager to undertake such action.

More complex and less autocratic organisations find it more difficult to change direction. It is noticeable that at times of crisis the industrial corporation tends to become more centralised and to move in a more authoritarian manner. In the past, the main casualties from rapid industrial change were manual workers, from the handloom weavers at the start of the industrial revolution, to the miners and shipyard workers in this century. They remain the main victims, both in numbers and in terms of the poverty inflicted. But the managerial classes, and those who articulate their beliefs, are perhaps now as deeply threatened both in economic and psychological terms by the threat of adverse business change.

The increasing difficulty that industrial organisations find in coping with change is bound up with the growth of new human relationships within the firm. Although the 1980s saw a reaction against employee participation and a reversion to more authoritarian styles of management, this seems likely to have been merely a temporary interruption in the underlying long-term trend. Indeed, the re-emergence of higher levels of unemployment will probably increase the importance most employees attach to job security, consultation and a sense of 'belonging' to the enterprise (just as the period of heavy unemployment between the wars dominated industrial attitudes in subsequent decades).

The climate of social opinion in Europe and North America is increasingly antagonistic towards arbitrary management action. Hence in evolving strategies to meet changing environmental conditions, firms are increasingly constrained by the need to have regard to the long-term interests of their employees. Management's inability to employ and lay off workers at will inhibits drastic expansion to meet any short-term upsurge in demand, as long as it seems in any danger of being reversed. It poses problems with running down the output of obsolescent products if

People and Change

new ones are to be produced elsewhere. Increasingly, firms will be faced with the problems of devising strategies that provide continuous employment for their staff despite changes in technology and economic conditions. If this is to be achieved whilst following a vigorous strategy of product development and response to market changes, most large firms (in the UK at any rate) face enormous strategic problems in the manpower field in establishing greater flexibility in working methods and long-term training. The distinctive threat to the industrial future of the UK is the combination of a high degree of social awareness and sensitivity to employment problems with a high degree of rigidity in working practices and training.

Strategy and Human Relations within the Firm

In his well-documented book, *Strategy and Structure*, Chandler developed the now accepted thesis that the organisation of the enterprise had to develop to match its strategy (although a more accurate deduction from the cases he examined would seem to be that a company's organisation developed to meet its operating needs, and such changes naturally followed some time after any new strategy was adopted).[2] The reverse is also true, however, namely, that the structure of an organisation influences its strategy: in particular, the vested interests of management in various decisions and functions have considerable weight in determining strategy. A further aspect of this proposition is now emerging, in that the structure of relations between the firm and its employees at all levels will become an increasingly important determinant of what is an acceptable strategy. A strategy which involves redundancies in one part of the organisation, new recruitment in another, and unacceptable changes in working practices in a third will not be consistent with maintaining the relationship between the company and its workers on which its ultimate success depends. This is a common enough fact of life in small companies or organisations, but it will become increasingly true in large-scale industry as well.

While the trade unions may articulate these feelings on behalf of their members, this trend runs over and above any growth or decline in unionism. Indeed, loyalty to trade unions spanning many firms within one or more industries has in a sense been a substitute for identification with a particular firm, and in the British situation may have prolonged the era in which employees did not expect to identify with their company and accepted uncertain employment. Strong craft unionism in the building trades, for example, is associated with relatively casual employment. Changes in the social climate are creating inexorable pressure for less hierarchical and more civilised human relations in industry irrespective of either trade union strength or the strength of demand for labour. Whereas the last major revolution in attitudes followed the growth in strength of organised labour with the advent of full employment in the Second World War and was fundamentally economic in origin, the trend now emerging is based more on changes in individual attitudes and the nature of work. For example, by 1983 a majority of employees in the UK were classified as 'white-collar' rather than manual workers. The new climate may be slower to appear while unemployment is high, and may become more rapidly manifest if unemployment falls.

These changes represent a challenge to the unions as well as employers. Employees will increasingly expect the unions to be orientated towards their firm rather than their industry as a whole, and this will lead to a trend against multi-union representation and towards single-union representation. Such changes and pressures will no doubt be slow and patchy, with considerable differences between industries; but the experience of Japanese companies setting up UK plants and seeking single-union agreements may be a catalyst.

Although the trend I am postulating corresponds in many respects to the way in which large companies have been operating in Japan, it is clearly no solution for British or American companies to attempt merely to copy Japanese ones – even though they have much to learn. In both Britain and North America the liberal ethic is still strong, and 'the actual quality of life in a business organisation turns most crucially on how much freedom is accorded to the individual.'[3] In Britain there are limitations on the extent to which most people are prepared to identify themselves wholly with the enterprise in which they work. On the other hand, the British have an almost insatiable desire to form societies or clubs, support teams and spend their time in like-minded groups. The problem is to harness this strong cultural tendency in a positive manner in large-scale industrial organisations.

Erosion of the concept of the standard working week to allow people to match their working hours to their changing personal and family circumstances should bring a new element of flexibility into firms' organisation. The fact that the same employees may work both 'full-time' and varying degrees of 'part-time' during their careers with a firm will in itself necessitate a periodic review of the work to be done, and how it should be organised. As this trend gets under way it will force enterprises to review and change their organisations. But firms which are prepared to take the trouble to marry the changing needs and availability of individuals to the work and responsibilities within the firm are likely to generate loyalty and enthusiasm. Thus taken together, the pressures for greater job security and greater flexibility in working time, can, if managed constructively, create stronger bonds of loyalty to the firm without creating excessive rigidity in the structure of employment.

Social Responsibilities

In so far as this diagnosis is correct, the increasing attention being paid by American management to external political and social factors may prove to have been a false start — in that their loss of world industrial leadership is a reflection of their inability to handle the internal social and human problems within the firm, rather than any lack of sensitivity to external pressures. It seems probable that any disillusion with the large American corporation has at least as much to do with life within the firm as with the corporation's failure to accept wider social responsibilities. In many ways top management's current concern with political and social leadership is nothing new: successful industrial leaders have always spent time on lobbying and the arts of political survival, and at the same time have wanted to cut a dash in a wider sphere. What is new is the inability to take the internal conditions of high productivity for granted.

The movement by some large American corporations (not yet noticeable in Britain) to assume wider social responsibilities should therefore be treated with caution. In addition to a longstanding tradition of providing financial support for university education, a few major American corporations have been concerned with such activities as city centre redevelopment, housing and schools. There is in a sense nothing new in this: the provision of infrastructure takes us back to the company town. In Britain, the trend has been strongly against, for example, the provision of housing by companies, partly for the practical difficulties in tied housing when someone changes his job, but more fundamentally as a reaction against the dominance of local communities by, for example, coal and steel owners. We look to democratically controlled bodies – central and local government – rather than large corporations to provide social services.

Moves to reverse this process have come from two directions. The first (seen in this country under Mrs Thatcher's government) is an attempt to limit the activity of government by arranging private provision of social services such as health care, or individual house ownership rather than local authority housing. The second is the provision of social services as a peripheral activity by industrial enterprises in order to make themselves more acceptable to the community. The latter movement (perhaps more significant philosophically than practically) on the other side of the Atlantic seems to reflect the feeling of a few large corporations that the great concentrations of power which they represent are vulnerable unless they are identified with more socially acceptable activities than their ordinary industrial ones.

If large corporations really did enter the provision of social services in any significant way, they would probably find (like government) that it is just as good a recipe for unpopularity as popularity. Moreover, the only rational way to enter into such activities is the slightly cynical one of doing something that will make the company look good. The public is very happy to see firms improve their public image by sponsoring sport, but they do not want the provision of vital services to become an adjunct of corporate image-building.

The Experience of Nationalised Industries

Undue emphasis on social objectives is in danger of leaving management with such an amorphous collection of objectives that it is no longer able to pursue any of them efficiently. The experience of the nationalised industries in the United Kingdom is pertinent here. Where for example, the railways tried to pursue social and industrial objectives in parallel, without any clear limit or price tag on their social objectives, the organisation tended to become inefficient and ineffectual.

The experience of the nationalised industries in their internal employee relations may also have some lessons for the private sector in adapting to these trends. The first lesson is that it is almost impossible to satisfy the aspirations of employees for a high degree of participation while struggling to achieve closures and redundancies. The experience of the British Steel Corporation in extending employee representation from Divisional boards to its main board demonstrated the tremendous strains placed on such a system when major closure decisions have to be taken.

The second is that it is impossible to provide security of employment in declining industries without the ability to diversify or introduce new products (or, failing that, securing alternative employment by some other means). Both the British Steel Corporation and the National Coal Board adopted much more generous early retirement provisions for their workforce than any private sector company in attempts to avoid compulsory redundancies. The Coal Board also made exceptional provisions for transferring miners to new pits, and the Steel Corporation pioneered efforts to bring new industry to steelmaking areas by setting up a special company, BSC (Industry) Limited, for this purpose.

Yet they both faced intense employee antagonism to their retrenchment plans.

The Trend Against 'Rationality'

The third (related) theme that academic writers on strategy have stressed recently is that less emphasis should be put on the 'rational' or analytical approach to strategy formulation. This is partly a reaction to the errors of quantitative forecasting that have been a feature of the last decade (see chapter 3); it is also a criticism of strategic plans built on elaborate quantitative analysis but containing basic assumptions that are implausible or have received insufficient scrutiny. Such a viewpoint is most easily provoked by a tendency to regard the right solution as determined by the best number to come out of the computer. Uncertainty, and the difficulty of quantifying human reactions, must always leave an area of judgement, however thorough the quantitative analysis. But the criticism should be one of the misuse of quantitative techniques, rather than of their use at all. The basic misuse is to pay too little attention to uncertainty.

It is perhaps salutary to quote the authors of *In Search of Excellence* before their emphasis of the importance of basic human factors becomes an excuse for abandoning proper analysis.

> The companies that we have called excellent are among the best at getting the numbers, analyzing them, and solving problems with them. Show us a company without a good fact base — a good quantitative picture of its customers, markets and competitors — and we will show you one in which priorities are set with the most byzantine of political manoeuvring. What we are against is wrong-headed analysis, analysis that is too complex to be useful and too unwieldy to be flexible, analysis that strives to be precise (especially at the wrong time) about the inherently unknowable ... [4]

Very often, a desire to avoid quantitative analysis merely reflects an unwillingness to face unpleasant facts.

The need is to establish a balance between the use of analytical methods to investigate a problem, the use of judgement to reach a decision on the action to be taken, and the emotional commitment to translate such a decision into successful action.

> The rational examination of alternatives and the determination of purpose are among the most neglected of all human activities. The final decision, which should be made as deliberately as possible after a detailed consideration of the issues we have attempted to separate, is an act of will and desire as much as of intellect.[5]

The Relevance for Strategy

What are the implications for business strategists in the 1990s?

First, the development of many enterprises' strategies will be constrained by changes in the structure of human relations within the firm, and must also be directed at achieving such changes. The nature of this change will include such developments as single status for manual and white-collar workers, wider discussion of problems at different levels, greater security of employment, greater flexibility of working at all levels and an acceptance of qualifications based on training in the course of working life. The need to achieve these changes internally will mean that personnel policy in its wider sense will be a major element in strategy. The constraints imposed by these developments will mean that strategies for product development and manufacturing must be in harmony with the pressures for greater job security and must exploit the greater flexibility of working and retraining that must go with it. Clearly in these circumstances, an increasingly decisive element in portfolio management and diversification strategy will be their impact on employees. Indeed, instead of such strategic decisions being those most remote from the workforce, they will tend to become closely linked to manpower policy.

There will also be repercussions on the way in which strategy is formulated and the purposes it serves. The less authoritarian the management style, the wider will be the field of discussion in determining strategy. It will become increasingly difficult to follow Stonewall Jackson's dictum, 'Mystify, mislead and surprise.' At the same time, the greater the interest of employees in the strategy of the enterprise, the more important will be its role in binding together people within the organisation and setting a common purpose and understanding of how it is to be achieved.

Notes

1 H. Igor Ansoff, *Strategic Management*, 1979, chapter 3.
2 Alfred D. Chandler, Jr, *Strategy and Structure: Chapters in the History of the American Enterprise*, 1962.
3 Kenneth R. Andrews, *The Concept of Corporate Strategy* (2nd edn), 1980.
4 Thomas J. Peters and Robert H. Waterman, Jr, *In Search of Excellence*, 1982, chapter 2.
5 Andrews, *The Concept of Corporate Strategy*.

Further Reading

Nearly all the various books and articles listed in the bibliography will be of interest to anybody wishing to pursue the subject in more detail. Students following a formal course on business policy will probably find it advisable to tackle one (but not more) of the many textbooks on the subject. These include:*

Lawrence R. Jauch and William F. Glueck, *Business Policy and Strategic Management*, (5th edn) 1988.

Charles W. Hofer and Dan Schendel, *Strategy Formulation: Analytical Concepts*, 1978.

Gerry Johnson and Kevan Scholes, *Exploring Corporate Strategy*, 2nd edn, 1988.

John A. Pearce II and Richard B. Robinson, Jr, *Formulation and Implementation of Competitive Strategy*, 1982.

George A. Steiner and John B. Miner, *Management Policy and Strategy*, 2nd edn 1982.

The second of these is probably the most complementary to this book, and is particularly strong on the portfolio approach.

For general reading, Kenneth R. Andrews, *The Concept of Corporate Strategy*, (2nd edn) 1980, is short, well-balanced and full of quotable wisdom. H. Igor Ansoff, *Corporate Strategy*, 1965, was in a sense a precursor of all that was to come and is still well worth reading, as in the collection of articles edited by him, *Business Strategy*, 1969.

The *Long Range Planning* journal published by Pergamon

---

* Works for which full publication information is not given are included in the bibliography.

for the Strategic Planning Society and the *Strategic Management Journal* (published by John Wiley) are the principal journals devoted specifically to business strategy and planning. The *Harvard Business Review* is also a mainspring of ideas in business policy.

Michael E. Porter, *Competitive Strategy*, 1980, is almost compulsory reading, particularly for anyone who wants to bridge the gap between the analytical approach of the economist and the prescriptive approach of the business strategist. Its sequel, *Competitive Advantage*, 1985, develops his prescriptions for successful strategies.

Books specifically devoted to planning (all of which cover much the same ground) include:

John Argenti, *Systematic Corporate Planning*, 1974.
David E. Hussey, *Introducing Corporate Planning*, 1979.
George A. Steiner, *Strategic Planning – What Every Manager Must Know*, 1979.

On diversification, Malcolm S. Salter and Wolf A. Weinhold, *Diversification through Acquisition*, 1979, is most useful.

A useful textbook on investment evaluation is Stephen Lumby, *Investment Appraisal*, London, Van Nostrand Reinhold, 1981.

For further reading on state enterprises see John Grieve Smith (ed.), *Strategic Planning in Nationalised Industries*, 1984.

The classic introduction to the relation between strategy and company organisation is Alfred D. Chandler, Jr, *Strategy and Structure: Chapters in the History of the American Enterprise*, 1962. A later, stimulating, study is Raymond E. Miles and Charles C. Snow, *Organisational Strategy, Structure and Process*, McGraw-Hill, 1978. Further interesting explanations of strategy and structure can be found in Toyohiro Kono, *Strategy and Structure of Japanese Enterprises*, 1984, and Michael Goold and Andrew Campbell, *Strategies and Styles*, 1987.

For those who are prepared to accept a high degree of

abstraction, two publications reflecting their author's reaction against conventional planning are: H. Igor Ansoff, *Strategic Management*, 1979, and Russell L. Ackoff, *Creating the Corporate Future*, 1981.

Among the many textbooks on statistics, J. J. Thomas, *An Introduction to Statistical Analysis for Economists*, 2nd edn 1983, is especially helpful on such topics as regression analysis.

Particularly interesting for the light it throws on the Japanese approach is: Kenichi Ohmae, *The Mind of the Strategist: Business Planning for Competitive Advantage*, 1983.

An excellent practical guide for new entrepreneurs is David Connell, *Starting a High Technology Company − Strategies for Success*, Deloitte Haskins and Sells High Technology Group and Barclays Bank, London, October 1985.

Select Bibliography

Ackoff, Russell L., *A Concept of Corporate Planning*, New York, John Wiley–Interscience, 1970.

Ackoff, Russell L., *Creating the Corporate Future*, New York, John Wiley, 1981.

Albert, Kenneth J., *The Strategic Management Handbook*, New York, McGraw-Hill, 1983.

Andrews, Kenneth R., *The Concept of Corporate Strategy* (2nd edn), Homewood, Illinois, Richard D. Irwin, 1980.

Ansoff, H. Igor, *Corporate Strategy*, New York, McGraw-Hill, 1965 and Penguin.

Ansoff, H. Igor (ed.), *Business Strategy: Selected Reading*, Harmondsworth, Penguin, 1969.

Ansoff, H. Igor, *Strategic Management*, New York, Macmillan, 1979.

Ansoff, H. Igor, *Implanting Strategic Management*, Englewood Cliffs, NJ, Prentice Hall, 1984.

Ansoff, H. Igor, Declerck, Roger P., and Hayes, Robert L. (eds), *From Strategic Planning to Strategic Management*, New York, John Wiley, 1976.

Argenti, John, *Systematic Corporate Planning*, London, Nelson/Van Nostrand Reinhold, 1974.

Argenti, John, *Corporate Collapse*, Maidenhead, Berks, McGraw-Hill, 1976.

Argenti, John, *Practical Corporate Planning*, London, Allen & Unwin, 1980.

Barksdale, Hiram, C., and Harris, Clyde E., Jr, 'Portfolio Analysis and the Product Life Cycle', *Long Range Planning*, December 1982.

Baynes, Peter, *Case Studies in Corporate Planning*, London, Pitman, 1973.

Beesley, M., and Littlechild, S., 'Privatisation: Principles, Problems and Priorities', *Lloyds Bank Review*, July 1983.

Beggs, James M., 'Leadership – The NASA Approach', *Long Range Planning*, April 1984.

Berle, Adolf A., and Means, Gardiner C., *The Modern Corporation and Private Property*, New York, Macmillan, 1932 (revised edn, New York, Harcourt, Brace & World, 1968).

Bettis, Richard A., 'Performance Differences in Related and Unrelated Diversified Firms', *Strategic Management Journal*, October–December 1981.

Bibeault, Donald B., *Corporate Turnaround: How Managers Turn Losers into Winners*, New York, McGraw-Hill, 1982.

Brown, James K., and O'Connor, Rochelle, *Planning and the Corporate Planning Director*, New York, The Conference Board, 1974.

Buzzell, R. D., Gale, B. T., and Sultan, R. G. M., 'Market Share – A Key to Profitability', *Harvard Business Review*, January–February 1975.

Buzzell, R. D., and Gale, B. T., *The PIMS Principles – Linking Strategy to Performance*, New York, Free Press, 1987.

Chandler, Alfred D., Jr, *Strategy and Structure: Chapters in the History of the American Enterprise*, Cambridge, MA, MIT Press, 1962.

Chandler, John, and Cockle, Paul, *Techniques of Scenario Planning*, Maidenhead, Berks, McGraw-Hill, 1982.

Chang, Yegmin, and Thomas, Howard, 'The Impact of Diversification Strategy on Risk – Return Performance', *Strategic Management Journal*, May–June 1989.

Channon, Derek F., *The Strategy and Structure of British Enterprise*, London, Macmillan, 1973.

Channon, Derek F., and Jallard, Michael, *Multinational Strategic Planning*, London, Macmillan, 1979.

Clifford, Donald K. Jr, and Cavanagh, Richard E., *The Winning Performance – How America's High-Growth Midsize Companies Succeed*, London, Sidgwick and Jackson, 1985.

Connell, David, *Starting A High Technology Company – Strategies for Success*, Deloitte, Haskins and Sells and Barclays Bank, London, October 1985.

Denning, Basil W. (ed.), *Corporate Planning: Selected Concepts*, Maidenhead, Berks, McGraw-Hill, 1971.

Drucker, Peter F., *Management*, New York, Harper's College Press and Pan Books, 1977.

Eggar, Robert F., and Menke, Michael M., 'An Inside View: Analysing Investment Strategies', *Planning Review*, May 1981 (reprinted in Milton Leontiades, ed., *Policy Strategy and Implementation: Reading and Cases*, New York, Random House, 1983).

Fildes, Robert, Jallard, Mike, and Wood, Douglas, 'Forecasting in Conditions of Uncertainty', *Long Range Planning*, August 1978.

Galbraith, John Kenneth, *The New Industrial State*, London, Hamish Hamilton and Penguin, 1967.

Gale, Bradley, T., and Branch, Ben, '"Allocating" Capital More Effectively', *Sloane Management Review*, fall 1987.

Goold, Michael, and Campbell, Andrew, *Strategies and Styles – The Role of the Centre in Managing Diversified Corporations*, Oxford, Basil Blackwell, 1987.

Grant, Robert M., and Jammine, Azar P., 'Performance Differences between the Wrigley/Rumelt Strategic Categories', *The Strategic Management Journal*, July–August 1989.

Grieve Smith, John (ed.), *Strategic Planning in Nationalised Industries*, London, Macmillan, 1984.

Griffith, Samuel B., *Sun Tzu: The Art of War*, Oxford, Oxford University Press, 1963.

Grinyer, Peter H., and Wooller, Jeff, *Corporate Models Today* (2nd edn), London, Institute of Chartered Accountants, 1978.

Handy, Charles, *The Age of Unreason*, London, Business Books, 1989.

Harrigan, K. R., *Strategies for Declining Industries*, Lexington, MA, D. C. Heath, 1980.

Hart, Sir Basil Henry Liddell, *Strategy: The Indirect Approach* (4th edn), London, Faber & Faber, 1967.

Hax, Arnoldo (ed.), *Readings on Strategic Management*, Cambridge, MA, Ballinger, 1984.

Hay, Donald A., and Morris, Derek J., *Industrial Economics, Theory and Evidence*, Oxford, Oxford University Press, 1979.

Hedley, Barry, 'A Fundamental Approach to Strategy Development', *Long Range Planning*, December 1976.

Hedley, Barry, 'Strategy and the Business Portfolio', *Long Range Planning*, February 1977.

Hofer, Charles W., and Schendel, Dan, *Strategy Formulation: Analytical Concepts*, St Paul, MN, West Publishing Co., 1978.

Hussey, David E., *Introducing Corporate Planning* (2nd edn), Oxford, Pergamon Press, 1979.

Hussey, David E., *Corporate Planning: Theory and Practice* (2nd edn), Oxford, Pergamon Press, 1982.

Jauch, Lawrence R., and Glueck, William F., *Business Policy and Strategy Management* (5th edn), Tokyo, McGraw-Hill Kogakusha, 1988.

Johnson, Gerry, and Scholes, Kevan, *Exploring Corporate Strategy*, (2nd edn), Englewood Cliffs, NJ, Prentice-Hall, 1988.

Kahn, Herman, and Wiener, Anthony, *The Year 2000*, New York, Macmillan, 1978.

Kay, John, Mayer, Colin, and Thompson, David (eds), *Privatisation and Regulation – the UK Experience*, Oxford, Clarendon Press, 1986.

Klein, Harold E., and Linneman, Robert E., 'The Use of Scenarios in Corporate Planning – Eight Case Histories', *Long Range Planning*, October 1981.

Kono, T., 'Long Range Planning of UK and Japanese Corporations – A Comparative Study', *Long Range Planning*, April 1984.

Kono, T., *Strategy and Structure of Japanese Enterprises*, London, Macmillan, 1984.

Kotler, Philip, Fahey, Liam, and Jatusripitak, Somkid, *The New Competition – What Theory Z Didn't Tell You About Marketing*, Englewood Cliffs, NJ, Prentice-Hall, 1985.

Leontiades, Milton, *Policy Strategy and Implementation: Readings and Cases*, New York, Random House, 1983.

Mason, Edward S. (ed.), *The Corporation in Modern Society*, Cambridge, MA, Harvard University Press, 1959.

Merritt, A. J., and Sykes, A., *Capital Budgeting and Company Finance* (2nd edn), London, Longman, 1973.

Merritt, A. J., *The Finance and Analysis of Capital Projects* (2nd edn), London, Longman, 1973.

Merritt, T. P., 'Forecasting the Future Business Environment: The State of the Art', *Long Range Planning*, June 1974.

Nationalised Industries White Papers:
    1961 (Cmnd 1337) *The Financial and Economic Obligations of the Nationalised Industries*, London, HMSO.
    1967 (Cmnd 3437) *Nationalised Industries: a Review of Economic and Financial Objectives*, London, HMSO.
    1978 (Cmnd 7131) *The Nationalised Industries*, London, HMSO.

O'Connor, Rochelle, *Multiple Scenarios and Contingency Planning*, New York, Conference Board Report No. 741, 1978.

Ohmae, Kenichi, *The Mind of the Strategist: Business Planning for Competitive Advantage*, Harmondsworth, Penguin, 1983.

Pascale, Richard Tanner, and Athos, Anthony, G., *The Art of Japanese Management*, Harmondsworth, Allen Lane and

Penguin, 1982.

Pearce, John A. II, and Robinson, Richard B., Jr, *Formulation and Implementation of Competitive Strategy*, Homewood, IL, Richard D. Irwin, 1982.

Peters, Thomas J., and Waterman, Robert H., Jr, *In Search of Excellence*, New York, Harper & Row, 1982.

Porter, Michael E., *Competitive Strategy*, New York, Free Press, 1980.

Porter, Michael E., *Competitive Advantage*, New York, Macmillan, 1985.

Prentice, J., 'Competing with Japanese Technology', *Long Range Planning*, April 1984.

Report of the Committee of Inquiry on Industrial Democracy ('Bullock Committee'), London, HMSO, January 1977.

Rumelt, Richard P., *Strategy, Structure and Economic Performance*, Cambridge, MA, Harvard University Press, 1974.

Rumelt, Richard P., 'Diversification Strategy and Profitability', *Strategic Management Journal*, October–December 1982.

Salter, Malcolm S., and Weinhold, Wolf A., *Diversification through Acquisition*, New York, Free Press, 1979.

Slatter, Stuart, *Corporate Recovery: Successful Turnaround Strategies and their Implementation*, Harmondsworth, Penguin, 1984.

Steiner, George A., *Strategic Planning – What Every Manager Must Know*, New York, Free Press, 1979.

Steiner, George A., 'The New Class of Chief Executive Officer', *Long Range Planning*, August 1981.

Steiner, George A., and Miner, John B., *Management Policy and Strategy* (2nd edn), New York, Macmillan, 1982.

Stone, M., 'Competing with Japan – The Rules of the Game', *Long Range Planning*, April 1984.

Suzuki, Y., 'The Strategy and Structure of Top 100 Japanese Industrial Enterprises, 1950–1970', *Strategic Management Journal*, July–September 1980.

Tavel, Charles, *The Third Industrial Age*, Oxford, Pergamon Press, 1980.

Taylor, Bernard, and Sparkes, John R., *Corporate Strategy and Planning*, London, Heinemann, 1977.

Taylor, Bernard, *et al.*, 'Scenarios for International Business', *Journal of General Management*, autumn 1981.

Thomas, J. J., *An Introduction to Statistical Analysis for Economists* (2nd edn), London, Weidenfeld and Nicolson, 1983.

Veljanovski, Cento, *Selling the State, Privatisation in Britain*, London, Weidenfeld and Nicolson, 1987.

Wack, Pierre, 'Unchartered Waters Ahead' and 'Shooting the Rapids', *Harvard Business Review*, September/October and November/December 1985.

Woo, Caroline Y., 'Evaluation of the Strategies and Performance of Low ROI Market Share Leaders', *Strategic Management Journal*, April–June 1983.

Woo, Caroline Y., and Cooper, Arnold C., 'Strategies of Effective Low Share Businesses', *Strategic Management Journal*, July–September 1981.

Index